D08843985

NATHANIEL MICKLEM

A Religion for Agnostics

SCM PRESS LTD
BLOOMSBURY STREET LONDON

FIRST PUBLISHED 1965
© SCM PRESS LTD 1965
PRINTED IN GREAT BRITAIN BY
BILLING AND SONS LTD
GUILDFORD AND LONDON

CONTENTS

	Preface	7
1	Science Must Be Atheist	17
2	The Evolutionary Process	29
3	Life Is Response	41
4	Religion	51
5	The Historical Question	64
6	Behind the Gospels	77
7	The Enigmatic Figure	89
8	The Vindication	101
9	An Intelligible Theology	114
10	Pain, Sin and Death	128
11	The World in Which I Live	143

PREFACE

A PREFACE should be at once an excuse and a sign-board. A writer owes the world, already overstocked with literature, an excuse or apology for adding yet another volume to the pile. Then as a matter of courtesy he should give a little sketch of the course he intends to run that those who foresee their lack of interest may be deterred from proceeding further.

First, then, my excuse and an appeal for patience. I have written for my friends, having now this one and now another in my mind, especially for those of my friends who either do not go to church or, if they do, are apt to come away wondering what, if anything, it is all about. My title is perhaps pretentious. Those who call themselves Agnostics (spelt with a capital letter) should be very learned men; to deserve their title they must have studied, so far as a man may, the story of human faith and speculation, have acquainted themselves with the deliverances of modern science, and must declare in the end that mortal man can have no certainties. I have used the word 'agnostic' in a humbler sense having in mind those many who wish they could be sure but have no confidence, no constant vision, whose spiritual life is a series of 'mere glimmerings and decays'.

In the pages that follow it is an argument that I offer, not a proof. I hope it may make appeal to those who are sensitive to more than material impressions, to whom music or

7

painting or poetry or religion or the beauty of Nature seems somehow 'shadowy of truth'. If any reader allow himself to suppose that I think myself to be offering some cogent proof, he will quickly be offended and be in the wrong frame of mind to treat me fairly. I think that my argument, for which I make no particular claims of originality, deserves the attention of serious and troubled minds. It is even in this sense, I believe, important in that it is what is today called 'existential', if I correctly understand the term. That is to say, the acceptance or rejection of it cannot be a merely intellectual judgment; it must be a decision of the whole person and must affect one's attitude to life at every turn.

Many of my friends complain that my books are (no doubt excellent but) 'difficult', and so, I fear, they are, being somewhat scholastic in language and technical in argument. I have been minded before I go, therefore, should time and strength be given to me, to put the gist of my more complicated arguments in the simplest terms. I have adopted, often to my personal discomfort, a familiar, repetitive, relaxed and even conversational style. I have been determined not to fall, except under the most extreme provocation, into Latin, still less to lapse into citations from the Greek. I plead, however, that one cannot write about faith and religion, still less about modern science, without using a few words unfamiliar on the Stock Exchange, in the public bar or in the shopping queue. Those who like their liquor less diluted may be referred to my writing, *Faith and Reason*.

Even so, nothing, I fear, can make my style acceptable and up to date. It may be said of me, as was said (more unkindly) of Mrs Piozzi, that I live 'in a perpetual state of rampant senility', and it is not possible for one who, long before the days of orange-juice and scientific gastronomy, was early nourished upon Plato and Cicero and Ruskin, to endure gladly or perpetuate willingly the literary ejaculations and explosions which are stylistically acceptable today. The kindly reader must put up with 'an insuppressible volubility of assertion'; he must be prepared to meander a little by the way, to pause here and there with me to admire the landscape, and, if he think fit, to light his pipe. I cannot write about religion, still less about God, in a hurry nor in staccato sentences. I can neither alter my manner of writing nor derive comfort by exclaiming with Charles Lamb, 'Damn the Age! I will write for Antiquity!', since it is those who live in this ambiguous and perplexed generation whom I would particularly address.

Perhaps my 'rampant senility' is not wholly to my disadvantage. 'If a body is not good-looking at twenty, nobody can blame her', wrote Peader O'Donnell in *The Big Windows*, 'but if she has not some share of good looks at sixty, she has only herself to blame; if God leaves her health.' Anyone of sixty seems young to me now, but God has left me health, and it would be sad if having lived through so many years, and having talked with so many interesting and even distinguished people, and having been required to give so many of my waking hours to the contemplation of those questions which ultimately matter most to human beings, I should have nothing to say as my days draw to a close or nothing that cannot be said quite simply. I write for those who are puzzled, and who is puzzled if not I? Yet if, as life goes on, the surrounding mysteries grow deeper, a few truths or intuitions or reasonable hopes become more luminous, and it is of these that I would write.

I have nothing to say here to those, be they materialists or Christians, who, fixed and rigid in their ideas, already know all the answers and are uncommonly zealous in their confident affirmations and denials. 'There is nothing in which men more deceive themselves', wrote Addison,[1] 'than in what the world calls zeal.' I admit that were it not from some inward excitement or zeal I should not have committed myself to these renewed labours of composition when I thought and hoped that my last book had been written; but over a wide and ever-extending field a wise and temperate agnosticism, as Christians in particular should remember, alone befits our mortal state. Yet man, as I judge, being almost incurably religious, cannot live happily or fruitfully without some faith; atheistic Communism is certainly a faith, though it would be wrong to call it a religion. In this new 'scientific' age, however, many or perhaps the majority of men live without any sense of spiritual security; tossed on the waves of circumstance and dazed by the discoveries of Science they 'fluctuate without term or scope'; at best they are hesitant half-believers in some ill-articulated creed. 'Chloe met his eyes gravely (I quote from Charles Williams' *Many Dimensions*); "I will remember," she said, "and—I do believe in God." "In spite of the fact that Giles Tumulty exists, so do I," Lord Arglay said, "though in a man of past fifty it's either an imbecility or a heroism." "And what for a girl of twenty-five?" Chloe asked. "O in her it's either a duty or a generosity," Lord Arglay said, "but for a secretary it's a safeguard. One must have something to explain or counter-balance one's employer! . . ."' '"Do you believe in God, Edward?" asks a character in Joyce Cary's *To Be a Pilgrim*. "Oh, yes, I believe in his existence. But how does one keep up one's interest in him?"' 'I was at that time living, like so many Atheists or Antitheists,' wrote C. S. Lewis of his unregenerate days, 'in a whirl of contradictions. I maintained that God did not exist. I was also very angry

[1] *The Spectator*, Octoer 2, 1711.

10

with God for not existing. I was equally angry with Him for creating a world."[1]

My departed friend, J. M. Thompson, wrote some years ago (he has found the answer now, I trust):

> I cannot love, but will not rail
> Against my maker; if he cares
> Whether I win or fail
> I cannot tell, nor how else fares
> The fight: only the harvester
> Knows how much wheat he sowed among the tares.[2]

Many, indeed, doubt whether there be any 'maker', any 'harvester', and here we must not look for any scientific confirmation or disproof. Yet which of us has not an instinctive sense that somehow 'in the masquerade of the grand carnival of our age,' to use Burke's phrase, there must somehow lie a meaning and a purpose?

> Believe thou, O my soul,
> Life is a vision, shadowy of Truth.

I must not be beguiled into a wistful anthology of modern hesitation and bewilderment. It is time to give an outline of the track I intend to follow. Science, I claim, can tell us nothing about ultimates; yet the scientist in various fields is aware of inscrutable Power, Intelligence and even Purpose. Matter, or that which used to be called matter, is as mysterious as is life. Out of matter or Nature there emerges man with his reason whereby he is able to grasp the universe as a whole, tracing its uniformities and recognizing it in some sense as a rational order, and with spiritual sensibilities such as a sense of beauty, an awareness of

---

[1] C. S. Lewis, *Surprised by Joy* (Bles, 1955) p. 113.
[2] In 'Elsfield', *Collected Verse 1939-1946* (Blackwell, 1947), p. 169.

obligation and a feeling for the ultimate or unconditioned. A limit to agnosticism is set by those intuitions which, however indemonstrable by logic, may not be denied without loss of personal integrity. Logic requires us to recognize a Power or Intelligence which may be called Nature or God, but there is no inevitable logical step from this recognition to religion, which is the apprehension of the Power not as an 'It', but as a 'Thou'. None the less, that non-material or spiritual environment which is the special endowment of the human species must be conceived in personal terms rather than impersonal.[1]

More fortunate readers who are concerned not with the question whether we may believe anything, but with the question what we rightly may believe, may be encouraged to leap directly to chapter 4, omitting those glimpses into the obvious (but often unobserved) which fill the earlier chapters. True religion will be man's right relationship to that spiritual world of which we all, as I think, are conscious, however dimly and however intermittently. Most of these later chapters are concerned with the figure of Jesus of Nazareth. I distinguish clearly between 'Christ' and 'Christianity' without wishing to speak ill of this or any other of the great religions of mankind. I have tried to indicate how centrally and crucially important in human history and our thought about religion is the figure of Jesus, to suggest in outline what may be accepted about him as of scientific historical accuracy, and to urge that his vindication is not a matter of historical or scientific proof but of intuition or of insight. We may remain agnostic to

---

[1] I am deeply grateful to my friend Dr Norman Spoor, of the U.K. Atomic Energy Authority, who in my early chapters dealing with scientific matters has saved me from many slips which an amateur is prone to make; but he is not to be held responsible for any errors or infelicities which may still remain.

the last, but I have tried to indicate those intuitions or insights which, as I believe, intellectual integrity requires, and not merely permits, us to trust for the regulation of our lives. In a final chapter I ask whether the pain, suffering and moral evil of the world in ages past as well as

> The present works of present man—
> A wild and dreamlike trade of blood and guile,
> Too foolish for a tear, too wicked for a smile . . .

are compatible with a conviction of the ultimate goodness of the universe and the compassionate heart of God to which the foregoing argument has pointed.

The epilogue is not part of the argument at all. Every such book as this must in a sense be autobiographical. My 'argument' is the record of my own engagement with many spectres of the mind and is my attempt to defend or justify on rational grounds that which I do not in the first instance believe because of any logic. In this epilogue I have tried to set forth where I stand after all the foregoing spectres have been laid. I have called my book *A Religion for Agnostics* because we must all be agnostic, confessing our great ignorance where men once were sure, but there must be limits to our agnosticism and uncertainty. There are some truths which we cannot demonstrate but cannot deny without despite to our manhood. We have 'intimations', as Wordsworth called them, or intuitions to which we must pay heed. We must renounce what Inge called 'the last infirmity of the philosophic mind—the desire to be invulnerable'. For myself, I stand midway—sometimes in discomfort—between those who claim to know more than mortal man can know and those, on the other side, who through some scrupulosity of the mind will not admit that which the heart knows very well.

13

Bernard Bosanquet, the philosopher, said, 'People who pray too much—it is an old folk-saying—pray themselves through heaven and out on the other side, and are set to herd geese there. People who ask too many questions, claiming to be religious in asking them—it seems much the same. . . . Science and logic have their rights, but we must not confuse them with religion. What a man's religion brings him, and what he cannot help receiving when he places himself humbly and sincerely in the attitude of religious faith, I should venture to suggest, let him hold to without scruple. It will be the nearest thing to truth that he can make his own.' Or perhaps my agnostic friends will like better this from Boris Pasternak: 'Facts don't exist until man puts into them something of his own, some measure of his own wilful, human genius—of fairy tale, or myth.' In this book I am not asking my agnostic friends to 'accept Christianity', a different theme. I am asking them to consider the significance for the whole human race of 'that strange Man upon his Cross'.

N.M.

Monks Staithe,
Princes Risborough.
February 1965.

P.S. This book, as I have said, was written for my friends. I had no thought that it would appear among these SCM Paperbacks. Perhaps it is just as well. I might have affected a more academic style had I known that I was writing for such readers. For the too frequent appearance of the first person singular alone I will apologize. But the two words 'I think' bear very different meanings according to the fall of the accent as they are spoken. When a speaker says '*I* think', he usually supposes his opinions to be important; when he says 'I *think*', he means that he ventures humbly to suggest. When in the following pages 'I think' or some similar phrase occurs, it will, I trust, be interpreted in the latter sense. I hope, indeed, that what I have written may by the indulgent reader be read not as a literary composition but as a very personal, and often very nearly private, conversation with my friends.

PUBLISHER'S NOTE

THE verses by Dr Micklem beginning 'Far off the eastern shores of Newfoundland' (p. 44), 'I never heard the larks so clear and sure' (p. 153) and 'Yet in his hand who lie' (p. 156) first appeared in *A Gallimaufry* (published by Bles, 1955). The second poem on p. 153, 'Ah, not all passes hence', is from *The Tree of Life* (Oxford University Press, 1952). We are grateful to the publishers for allowing these lines to appear again in the present book.

1

SCIENCE MUST BE ATHEIST

THE word 'Science', spelt with a capital letter, is a vague and abstract term, in popular speech often virtually personified as some great lady bountiful, exacting, wise, as when men say that Science teaches this, Science demands that, or Science is impatient of something else. There are in fact many sciences, and there is much scientific knowledge, but there is no such being or entity as Science. This general term, however, is most convenient, and I have not hesitated to employ it, meaning thereby the methods and findings of scientific enquiry in any field.

When I head my chapter 'Science must be atheist', I mean not that all scientists are, or should be, atheists, but that the existence or Being of God is not a question relevant to scientific studies. In prescientific days it was customary to ascribe to God or to the gods any occurrence for which man could see no natural cause. Divine intervention was invoked to fill up those gaps in human understanding which with the advance of modern Science grow ever less and less. The inexplicable is for Science that which has not yet been explained; its ideal is to leave no gaps. For a physicist, a chemist or a biologist as such, therefore, it would be as improper to ascribe an event to divine intervention as it would be for the scientific historian to break into his account of a campaign with the observation that at this point or that God interposed his hand to rout the enemy.

It is the task of Science to describe the world in which we live, and then, so far as possible, to subsume all events under general laws and principles. The purpose of those experiments upon which modern Science largely rests is first to see what happens and then, if possible, to reach some hypothesis which will account for this result. There are, as is well known, 'freaks' in nature, but no scientist will invoke the name of God to account for freaks. Every scientist sees the universe as a vast system of 'laws' or uniformities. This event, he says very properly, is 'caused' by that. Why does the sun 'rise' in the morning and 'sink' at nightfall? Why do the tides of the ocean ebb and flow? Why does it hurt to poke one's finger in the fire? Because Science can answer ever more questions of this kind, it has made possible the marvellous technical advances of the modern world. In all these enquiries and in all these discoveries it is unnecessary and indeed improper to invoke the name of God. Science is by its very nature a-theist, and because we all, however amateurishly, think scientifically today, religion is apt to seem remote, irrelevant, unreal.

At a deeper level, it is true, the scientist never answers the question why. He tells us that water may be prepared by an interaction between two volumes of hydrogen and one of oxygen, but if we should be so unkind as to ask him further why this particular interaction between hydrogen and oxygen should produce something wet, he will shrug his shoulders and tell us compassionately or irritably that it is his business to explain the world as it happens to be, not to explain why it is what it is. If, I may add, the theologian should here chip in with the observation that this happens because God wills it, he has done nothing whatever to elucidate the mystery.

I see that I am coming now to ideas which in spite of the promises of my preface must be called 'difficult'. They

18

are difficult, however, not because any scientific experience or grasp of philosophic principles is needed for their understanding but because they put so great a strain upon our imagination.

Science deals with the physical or material world which impinges on our senses. It cannot deal with our thoughts, our secret aspirations, our ecstasies, our sufferings, for these belong to a private and personal world beyond its scope. There are those who say that this latter, inward world, beyond the reach of scientific experiment, is unreal, though it seem very real to us. This is a hazardous hypothesis to which we shall return. I am not here quite forgetting that psychology and sociology and politics and ethics, claiming to be sciences, deal with the inward movements of the human spirit, but they bring us all under general laws and must forget our differences. The universe contemplated by Science, as we usually understand the term, includes the sun and the galaxies, the earth and everything we see and touch, our eyes and ears, our hands and feet, our nerves and brains and all revealed by microscope or spectroscope. All these we call material things. What then is matter?

The early scientist-philosophers among the Greeks supposed that earth or air or fire or water is the ultimate component of all things. Soon there arose the theory of atoms which is enshrined in the magnificent poem of Lucretius. Indeed, down to quite recent times it was supposed that the ultimate constituents of all material objects are little solid particles called atoms. 'Atom' means by derivation that which cannot be divided; the atom was the ultimate indivisible unity from which all objects are constructed. In these last days we have split the atom, exploded all the ancient theories, and are in much danger of blowing up ourselves as well. The old-fashioned crude materialism of the nineteenth century is held by no educated man today, and when the disciples of Karl Marx call themselves materialists, we must not suppose them to be bad scientists. What, then, is matter to the modern scientist?

I suppose that such a man in his scientific work never speaks or thinks of 'matter'; but when we ask him of what this physical or material world of ours is ultimately composed, he gives us an answer which makes sense and is the result of marvellous experiments, but he tells of that which neither he nor we can picture or imagine or claim to understand. He will expatiate upon 'electrons' of unimaginable velocity and not wholly predictable behaviour. What is an electron? I think there is no answer. It is much too simple to say that it is an electric somewhat, for we do not know what electricity *is*, we only know what it will do; it is a name for that which happens. Nor may we properly speak of an electron as a somewhat as if it were a thing. Sometimes scientists speak of it as if it were a particle, sometimes as if it were a wave; it is neither quite one nor quite the other. An electron, therefore, is an entity which scientists must postulate but cannot picture or imagine. This does not imply that the electron does not in some sense exist, still less that the scientists are talking nonsense. They say to us, in effect, 'In order to account for that which we know of the world by experiment we have to postulate mysterious entities with certain properties which we have agreed to call electrons.' They can go no further, but at no point in their enquiries and experiments have they had occasion to introduce the name or the hypothesis of God.[1]

I come to an even greater strain on our imagination. It is we ourselves who create the universe of which our senses

[1] A recent and relatively popular account of where the physicists now stand will be found in J. R. Oppenheimer, *The Flying Trapeze: Three Crises for Physicists* (Oxford University Press, 1964).

give us evidence. This monstrous paradox I must now seek to explain.

When I look through the window into my garden this morning, I can see yellow aconites, white snowdrops and the first purple of the budding crocuses. What would be the scientific account of this enheartening experience? From aconites, snowdrops, crocuses, the scientist will say, there proceed in my direction what he calls 'light-waves'; their velocities or vibrations may correspond with colours, but of themselves they are not coloured. These light-waves, however they be conceived, strike upon the receptive retina of my eye and set up thence a series of electric currents which impinge upon my brain. These currents certainly are not coloured, nor are there any portions of my brain that are appropriately coloured yellow, white and purple. Yet by a process which is as incomprehensible as it is familiar I see these flowers as coloured. Do the light-waves and the electric currents and the brain operations enable me to see the colours that are really there upon the flowers? The flowers, we are told, are collocations or constellations of different molecules, which Science may further reduce to atoms and sub-atomic particles. These invisible particles are not things which can be pictured; indeed, they are not strictly *things* at all but, rather, hypothetical and non-material entities postulated by our present state of knowledge. It is my own mind, therefore, which creates the colours which I see. On the other hand, it is certainly not I who make the aconite yellow, the snowdrop white and the crocus purple, for were my present reader standing by my side, he would see these colours too and share my pleasure, unless, indeed, he happen to be colour-blind.

Let me take one further illustration: the material, physical world of which we are aware consists very largely of

21

solid objects. The table upon which my typewriter is resting, for instance, is indubitably solid. By the exercise of much force and patience I might with a bradawl make a hole in it, but only by violently forcing asunder the particles which cohere to make it solid. I see, I feel, I experience my table as a solid object. To the physicist, however, it is an association of nucleons and electrons with relatively vast spaces between each. It is, in fact, more like the solar system than a solid object. The table I apprehend or experience as solid; it is solid enough to me, but in itself, from the scientific point of view, it is by no means solid. It is I, or, rather, it is we human beings to whom it is solid, who make it solid.

I am writing of that of which, when we think, we are familiar: we know the world as coloured and as solid, but 'really' or underneath or behind this opaque, solid world of our experience there are only transparent and largely vacuous constellations of nucleons and electrons. No wonder modern man feels dizzy, uncertain, lost in such a paradoxical situation. The great significance of this for religion he has rarely glimpsed.

Let me put one further strain upon imagination by a necessary consideration which, I suppose, is philosophic rather than strictly scientific. The geologists and archaeologically-minded botanists describe to us pre-history, the story of this planet before man or even animals appeared upon it. What they tell us, however, is not what happened but what *we* should have *seen* had *we* been present. What we should have seen would have been a seething of waters, an up-throwing of great mountains, the gradual formation of river beds, the later peeping of greenery upon the mud-flats. But in fact there was no observer there, and in the absence of an observer, it is meaningless to speak of here or there, of near or far, of long or short, of fast or slow, of light or dark. What was there from the scientific point of view were collisions and conglomerations, a whirling and a swirling of electrons, though the philosopher or scientist, to be sure, is at liberty to assume or infer that there were photosynthesis and enzymes and chromosomes and all the other complicated biochemical paraphernalia which we have learnt to associate with 'life'. In this very important sense it is we human beings, through our senses, who create the world which we experience.

To make matters worse, or at least more complicated and more puzzling, the scientists now assure us that our weights and measurements, though conveniently stable for all practical purposes, have no absolute validity. For instance, a yardstick we say is precisely a yard long; all objects, therefore, which are of the same length as that stick will be of identical length with one another. In view of the experiments and discoveries of Einstein and others, we have now to understand that if the yardstick be travelling at a sufficient velocity, its length will be appreciably reduced. That is to say, an object which is of identical length with the yardstick when the latter is at rest will not be of the same length as another object which is of identical length with that yardstick travelling nearly as fast as light. Or again, if my reader were sitting comfortably on earth while I was travelling in an aeroplane at 99.5 per cent of the speed of light, the clock in my aeroplane would move one minute forward while the reader's clock would mark the passage of ten minutes. What would 'the right time' be? Worse still for me, if my aeroplane so accelerated as to attain the speed of light, the scientists tell me it would cease to be a solid object and itself become light or, as they would put it, energy; what would become of me they cannot tell! As for my clock, if (by some miracle or rather impossibility) it had not disintegrated into light or energy

23

with the aeroplane, it would not have stopped, but the hands would not move, for time itself would have stopped. Our weights, our measures and our time are only relative or relatively stable!

I have laid stress upon these elementary and familiar data of modern Science for three reasons. First, they go far to account for the desolating uncertainty and insecurity which afflicts the human spirit in these days. Second, I would make full admission that those who call themselves materialists or atheists are wholly justified in their claim that, while Science as it advances is giving us an ever wider and fuller account of the universe in which we live, there is no point at which Science has to invoke the name of God to give an explanation of events. Science, when it is true to itself, is and must be a-theist. Third, it has been customary to contrast this solid, objective, material world which we know by our senses with the insubstantial subjective world of art, of imagination, of religion which lacks the assured 'reality' of the material world. Whether there be any 'reality' at all in the world of poetry, of myth and of religion is a question to which we shall come later, but we should recognize that Science as it has advanced, has rendered curiously insubstantial or even 'unreal' this visible, tangible world of our sensible experience. 'Matter' of which we say all things are composed becomes itself by the experiments of the scientists both shadowy and immaterial; our weights and our measures, however satisfactory and sure for practical purposes, have only relative validity; time depends on speed, and in large measure we ourselves create the world which we experience. There is no matter, said A. N. Whitehead; there are no substances; there are events; and events, I take it, receive their significance through the eye of the beholder and his insight. Many have thought that modern Science has taken away our God; it is much more certain

24

that it has taken away our once so assured, so solid and so measurable earth.

Before there was an observer, I said, we could only conceive of the universe as a whirling conglomeration or collision of electrons. These supposed electrons, however, constituted not a chaos but an order. 'Laws', such as the so-called 'laws of thermodynamics', held good for them; there were unchanging regularities of behaviour such as the four hundred and fifty rotations achieved, I am told, by a molecule of hydrogen every second; patterns were emerging such as the crystal or the snowflake. If we ourselves must be said to create the colours and the solidity of the world of our experience, we certainly do not create the mathematical uniformities which modern Science has discovered. The aim of the scientist is to bring an ever-increasing number of discoveries under some wider mathematical formula, and Sir James Jeans, not very felicitously, suggested that God might be regarded as the great Mathematician in some superior sense. 'The driving force in Philosophy', said C. C. J. Webb (and here we may substitute Science for Philosophy), 'is the passion for unity as in Aristotle's contemplation of the unmoved Mover or Spinoza's intellectual love of God, the love consisting in understanding of that perfect and all-comprehending system which he calls indifferently Nature or God.'[1] Many may be asking themselves in these days whether 'God' is but a pious and emotional name for Nature.

Tossing a halfpenny I might find that ten times successively it might by chance turn up heads; dropping an open ink-pot on the carpet I might by chance produce an exceeding regrettable but otherwise very pretty pattern. But the patterns and the kind of order which the scientists discover in the universe cannot sensibly be ascribed to chance.

[1] *Pascal's Philosophy of Religion*, 1929, p. 32.

It may be by chance that any particular acorn should fall into the hedgerow and there grow into a tree, but it cannot be by chance that every oak bears acorns, and each acorn has in it the potentiality to become an oak. Science has to presuppose an order and uniformity in the world it studies, and this presupposition is verified by observation and experiment. Science, then, is dealing with an order, not a chaos.

In its new-found twentieth-century humility Science is disposed to speak rather of 'averages' than of 'laws', but in its search for, and its discovery of, the uniformities expressed in mathematical formulae of ever greater scope it rests wholly upon the presupposition that the universe is a rational order to be explored by the rational faculties of man. But rationality is the correlative of intelligence. This universe being no merely chance affair, Mind, as Professor Stout said, 'is not produced at all, but is in some way involved as a primary factor in the creation of the universe.'[1] It would be quite illegitimate at this point of the argument for a triumphant theologian to claim that here we read the Mind of a personal God. This was the traditional 'argument from design', which has a long history in Christian thought. 'For my own part', writes Professor W. A. Whitehouse, 'I subscribe to the widely held view that any such argument, even if it could be formulated and sustained, would be technically useless. It would do nothing to reduce the obscurity of what it purports to explain.'[2] It cannot well be denied, however, that the order which we find and study in the universe necessarily involves something corresponding or analogous to intelligence.

[1] Quoted by W. Macneile Dixon, *The Human Situation* (Penguin ed., 1958), p. 314.
[2] W. A. Whitehouse, *Order, Goodness, Glory* (Oxford University Press, 1960), p. 27.

That which is rational cannot be meaningless; it must be related to some purpose. Here, however, we must be very careful. It is one thing to claim that the order of the universe must, at least according to our human way of thinking, bear within itself a meaning or a purpose; it would be quite another thing to claim that we have any inkling of what that meaning or that purpose is. By those whose ideas were derived from the Bible it was for generations supposed that the world was created and exists for the sake of man upon this planet. Such a view is no longer tenable. If the theologian cares to assert that God made the Milky Way, he is in no position to answer the question why God made it or what purpose it may be supposed to serve. Agnosticism, which denotes an admitted ignorance, is increased with every advance of knowledge. We are bound, however, to say that the universe which Science explores and expounds as a cosmic, coherent order must have some rational Ground on which it rests.

At this point I am somewhat at a stand. The term 'Ground' has been made familiar to us in recent years by Professor Paul Tillich, but 'rational Ground' is what the grammarians call an oxymoron, the conjunction of two contradictory terms. Other writers use various words, such as Matter, Nature, God, to indicate that which Tillich has called Ground, but to all these also there is objection. 'Matter' is nowadays not merely too solid but is not even a very scientific term; 'rational Matter' is as difficult as is 'rational Ground'. 'Nature' might seem better, but Dame Nature or Mother Nature with her various gifts, her shifting moods and spendthrift prodigality is, after all, a figure of mythology; and 'God' is a religious word which is inappropriate to my present argument. I therefore gratefully fall back upon a phrase in Margaret Murray's *My First Hundred Years* (p. 204), where she speaks of 'that great

27

Power, which science calls Nature and religion calls God'.
I shall prefer the term Power then, or rational Power,
vague though it be, because I think it will be accepted alike
by theists and by atheists, being applicable either to an
electron or to God.

'Before the eternal silence of these infinite spaces I am
afraid,' wrote Pascal in a famous passage ('*Le silence
éternal de ces espaces infinis m'effraie*'). Modern man,
when he stops to think, participates in this cosmic terror.
We know of nebulae, I am told, which are a hundred
million light-years from us. I will not claim to believe this
or be able to imagine it, but it may be so, and if the
astronomers assert it as a fact, I must accept it. There have
been times, as in the Middle Ages, when man could feel at
home in a tidy and comfortable universe around him; today,
assured of these unimaginable immensities of space and time
and of the infinitesimals of molecular science, when the
very solidity of matter has been taken from him and his
most careful measurements are proved ultimately invalid,
he feels himself homeless, dizzy, shelterless. The universe
as an expression of Intelligence does not scare him, for it is
answered or partially reflected in his own intelligence, but
a sense of the Power that formed and rules the nebulae and
the galaxies, that is hidden within the atom, terrifies him.
Science describes all this for him without any need or
occasion to mention God, and, indeed, what God could
be here revealed to comfort him? No wonder modern man
is lonely, afraid and lost.

2

THE EVOLUTIONARY PROCESS

THE universe as explored by Science is not merely an order as distinct from a chaos; it is manifestly a vast process also. Here, when we settle down to think of it, we are met by an insoluble perplexity or contradiction. A process to our thinking must have a beginning and an end. A universe, we think, must have a beginning in time and an ending in space, but we cannot imagine time beginning or space ending, for there must have been half an hour before the beginning of time and a yard beyond the end of space. We can torture ourselves with these vain attempts to think that which cannot be thought. The scientist cannot help us here, nor is the theologian in any better case. It is easy for the latter to say that in the beginning God created the world out of nothing and will reduce it to nothing in the end, but it is not possible to attach any clear meaning to these phrases. We must be content to say that all human experience of the universe is in terms of time and space and leave the matter there. We must say, however, that the universe, because it is an order, must have some Ground and, because it is a process, must be the expression of some Power and, because it is to be apprehended by reason, it must serve some meaning or significance.

We may not claim that a particular process must necessarily have a purpose. Astronomers tell us of stars which have come to be and then exploded. What purpose, if any, they may have served we cannot conjecture. The Milky Way rides there in the sky

Set for a wonder, silent for an awe,

but we cannot suppose that its sole or primary purpose is the excitation of emotions in the human breast. Rational order is one thing; purpose is another.

But when we descend to our own planet of which alone we have some intimate knowledge, the biologists reveal to us manifest signs not merely of intelligence, but also of conation or purposive effort in an evolving order. 'Living matter', writes Professor Whitehouse, 'exhibits self-regulating processes, leading to an organism with a definite structural and functional character.'[1] When a pair of swallows build their nest beneath the eaves, their activity is clearly purposeful. We dare not assume that as they work they consciously foresee the eggs and fledglings which, if all goes well, will find their home there. In the autumn, gathering with their fellows, they will start on their prodigious but sure flight to Africa, next spring to return across unnumbered miles to the familiar eaves. It is said that pigeons, loosed from a ship in mid-Atlantic, have found their way across a thousand miles of trackless sea in a straight line to their home. What thoughts, if any, or vague consciousness enter the minds of these birds we cannot tell; they act instinctively, but herein they act intelligently even if we cannot ascribe the intelligence to them.

Or we might consider the making of the spider's web. An eminent observer described to Charles Raven the perfection of the process, 'the choice of the site and the planning of the periphery, then the commencement within it of the web proper, the measuring off and laying down of the main radii, the insertion of symmetrical subsidiary radii, and finally the filling up of the connecting lines linking them together. He declared that both in the quality of its pattern

[1] *Order, Goodness, Glory*, p. 44.

30

and in the economy and ingenuity of its construction it was an *opus perfectum*, such as no geometer, however expert, could improve upon: indeed, over some of the details like the technique of the bridging he, a man not given to easy praise, became almost lyrical in his admiration."[1] This expert observer went on to explain, however, that though the spider could construct a faultless web it had no understanding of its own operation, for if the web were injured and in need of repair, the work was 'botched as badly as a man's darning of a sock'. He was convinced, after long and careful observation, that 'neither the present spiders of this species nor their ancestors were ever the architects of the web, or that it could conceivably have been produced step by step through random variation.'

One of the many marvellous intricacies of Nature is that mechanism whereby so many living creatures see. I read[2] that the eye of a butterfly contains five thousand lenses and no less than fifty thousand nerves, that the retina of the human eye can, as it were, distinguish between light-vibrations, whatever they may be, of four hundred and fifty million millions a second and those of seven hundred and fifty million millions a second, the mind interpreting the former as redness, the latter as violet. Many creatures have eyes, but not all have developed eyes in the same way nor from the same part of the body. And how, we may ask, is our eye produced? The germ-cells which come together to form the human body are not specialized for the functions they are to perform, and each, it appears, if it is injured, is able out of any part of itself to produce any necessary organ, the eye or any other. The human body

[1] C. E. Raven, *Natural Religion and Christian Theology:* Gifford Lectures, second series, 'Experience and Interpretation' (Cambridge University Press, 1953), p. 136.

[2] W. Macneile Dixon, *The Human Situation*, pp. 140 f.

with its parts and organs is an astounding marvel of co-operation on the part of living cells.

'This co-operation of parts', wrote Macneile Dixon, 'is everywhere present in natural organisms. What governs the procedure? Who or what presides over the organization? Where dwells the wisdom in the germ capable of detecting deficiencies in itself when they arise, where the intelligence for it certainly simulates intelligence, which can transfer to the remaining parts duties previously performed by others? . . . This pinpoint of matter which the physicists . . . analyse for you, as they do all substances, into spinning charges of electric energy, this speck of life, which is a whirlwind of billions of electrons, revolving in their orbits about seven thousand million times in the millionth of a second—contains within itself the power of becoming a human being, with all its organs complete, brain, heart and lungs . . . It contains within itself the power of repro-ducing its kind, of recalling the features, the smile, the complexion, the trick of speech, the grace of carriage that characterize the parent stock. This speck of matter contains within itself these noteworthy powers.'

Being neither a biologist nor a physicist, I accept these facts with an almost incredulous wonder, but only Dixon's conclusion—'this speck of matter contains within itself these noteworthy powers'—is perhaps avoidable. Matter the physicists have reduced to nucleons and electrons and a variety of sub-atomic particles which we can neither picture nor imagine; if we now have to ascribe to them or to some of them the faculty of producing cells which are themselves intelligent and capable of the most intricate co-operation with one another, we make the mystery of 'matter' yet more baffling.

The phrase 'the survival of the fittest'. made familiar by Herbert Spencer, points to a very important element in the evolution of life upon this planet, but it is not adopted or accepted by the scientists. In the first place, it introduces a term of valuation, and Science is concerned with facts and 'laws', not values. In the second, it suggests, though it is not intended to assert, that all Nature is a battle-ground. Such it is, no doubt, in part, for the depredations, the cruelties, the massacres inflicted by man on man in history have their a-moral counterpart elsewhere in the struggle for survival. But, more significantly and more profoundly, Nature, as scientists study it on our earth, represents a vast and immensely complicated system of balance and inter-dependence and co-operation of interrelated parts wherein soil, air, water and all animal life combine to create a mysterious harmony or whole.

A scientist may care to ascribe these marvels of mathe-matical order, or purposive action and fabulous skill to 'Nature' or to 'Matter'.[1] If so, he is assuming a mythological

[1] In self-defence, and to my great regret, I must here insert a footnote which let him omit who will. The biologists do not ascribe to 'Nature' or to 'Matter' the evolutionary order which they study. The term they use is 'natural selection', a term which is for them convenient shorthand but which I am bound to avoid because of its grievous ambiguity. Dr David Lack, F.R.S., tells us in his book *Evolutionary Theory and Christian Belief: the Unresolved Conflict* (Methuen, 1957) that no biologist believes any longer in a Life Force (p. 54). The idea of Creative Evolution is likewise to be rejected (p. 57), with the traditional argument from Design (p. 75). Natural selection is to be contrasted with 'a guiding rational or spiritual influence in evolution'; it aims only at survival (p. 59); it is a-moral (p. 108); it is 'the main agent of evolutionary change' (p. 48); it operates upon 'heritable tendencies' (p. 102). Evolution, so far as is known, takes place only in terms of 'the natural selection of hereditary variations' (p. 113). Natural selection is, in fact, 'the means of evolution' (p. 103).

Now in so far as this theory provides a rational *description* of the evolutionary process, it is both illuminating and strictly scien-tific. Dr Lack quotes an instance where natural selection was

background in his thinking, for strictly 'Nature' is as much a mythological figure as the Mother-goddess, and 'Matter' itself belongs to mythology if to it be ascribed these plans and purposes and astonishing achievements. Atheistic scientists, no less than theists, must recognize in the universe Intelligence and Power and Purpose. The difference between them is that the atheist, avoiding the name of God, conceives this Power as wholly immanent within the universe, whereas the theist believes in a transcendent God beyond the universe. The atheist is involved in a mythology of 'Nature'; we must later consider whether a transcendent God is not likewise a Being of mythology.

It is only atheistic scientists, declaring with supreme assurance that there is no God, who must lapse inevitably into the new mythology. In general, the great men of science know far too much to know that there is no God. Lord Rosebery, addressing the University of Glasgow, spoke of Lord Kelvin's tenacity and laboriousness and indefatigable humility, his lack of superciliousness or scorn of others: 'without condescension he placed himself at once on a level with his companion. That has seemed to me a characteristic of such great men of science as I have chanced to meet. They are always face to face with the

---

'caused by birds' (p. 45). But if the theory is merely descriptive, the term 'selection' is unfortunate, and in fact we find that natural selection, which here should surely be spelt with capitals, is 'an agent' (p. 53); it is 'a conservative force' (p. 46); it 'operates' (p. 102); it 'requires a high death-rate' (p. 76); it 'favours' this or that evolution; it is, in fact, a force or power that actually selects. But who or what selects? A disembodied rational force that operates as or upon or within Nature belongs, I think, to mythology, not Science. The phrase 'natural selection' suggests that it is Nature which selects. In the text, therefore, I have avoided the ambiguous term 'natural selection'. (See further *Nature and God* by Professor L. Charles Birch SCM Press, 1965.)

transcendent mysteries of nature; they stand on the high mountain apart and are themselves transfigured by what they witness: penetrated with the awe of that communion, they shed, as it were unconsciously, the petty pride of man, and shine with the humility of real knowledge. Who can be presumptuous who lives in a firmament of worlds, and deals with the unbounded problems of space and time? Such labours produce a sublime calm, and it was that which was always to pervade Lord Kelvin.'[1] The reverent agnosticism of a great scientist may be far more deeply religious than the glib assurance of those who lightly and familiarly take upon their lips the name of God.

The world is an order; the scientists study its 'laws' or uniformities; but it is not a mechanical order. When an event has occurred, we can always see why it was bound to occur; but this does not enable us to predict with absolute certainty what will occur. Within this order, and in spite of these uniformities, there is room for the contingent, the unexpected, the unpredictable, the new; there is an element of freedom (or what looks like freedom) within the order. It is not merely that when human choice must be taken into account, there is an element of uncertainty, for the electrons themselves, as physicists at present suppose, sometimes behave in quite unexpected ways.[2] The biologists must reckon 'with the random mutation of genes'. The world, especially as we can study it at close quarters on this planet of ours, does not seem to resemble a machine that is not quite predictable because it goes wrong sometimes; it is much more like a machine (if we can imagine such) which every now and then would right itself

---

[1] Lord Rosebery, *Miscellanies* (1921), Vol. II, pp. 135 ff.

[2] The quantum theory, says Dr Oppenheimer, is a 'non-determinist theory'. He write of a 'spontaneous' transition within the atom (*The Flying Trapeze*, pp. 43, 53).

or improve itself and then stay right or improved. It is as if Nature were a being of illimitable patience making experiments which after countless ages in the end succeed. First molecules cohere ('learn to cohere', I had almost said); then land and sea become separate; protoplasm appears; out of the slime emerge creatures which in the end develop into fish, animals, reptiles, birds in their various and numerous genera and species; then man arrives with his gradually developing civilization and appreciation of the beautiful, the good, the true. Evolution might be represented as a groping, a blind and yet somehow a guided groping, and it is open to scientists to accept the suggestion that some sort of scarcely imaginable embryonic consciousness runs through the universe, that there is a conative or dimly explorative element in matter itself, that the distinction between the organic and the inorganic is not absolute.

We have yet to consider the most startling product of the evolutionary order. The mystery of rational man remains the same whether we ascribe his origin to 'Nature' or to 'Matter' or to 'God'. Out of the evolving order there issues a being who recognizes it for an evolving order. Nature produces man, yet in another sense Nature herself is man's creation, for 'Nature' is a mental concept, and no animal, so far as we can judge, has any idea of Nature as a whole, still less of Nature as a ceaseless ballet of whirling protons and electrons. Man belongs to the animal creation, and yet not altogether. He is a new thing in the story of Evolution. He not only knows but he also knows that he knows; he is as one with a foot in two worlds, who both arises out of Nature and stands over against Nature in contemplation of it. Man is, in the happy phrase of Sir Thomas Browne, 'that amphibious piece between a corporal and a spiritual Essence'. We may not claim to understand the psychology of animals, but we are sure that no animal cries out with Pascal, 'Before the eternal silence of these infinite spaces I am afraid.' Animals are at home in the world, with instinct for their guide; it is only man who knows a cosmic fear, who is unsure of himself, lonely and lost amid the immensities that surround him. Man not only feels and instinctively responds, he speculates, he dreams, he prays.

He prays. I do not mean that most men normally 'say their prayers'. I am only pointing to the indubitable fact that in the natural order and in the course of Evolution there has arisen a creature whose mind is not limited to the little area presented by the senses, but ranges over the whole realm of being, analyses its nature, notes its process, declares its beauty, and passing beyond the world of visible things raises the question of that which lies beyond, and who has been accustomed to address himself in prayer to the Power or powers which superintend, as he supposes, the world of sensible phenomena. I do not claim that this is true of every man. Very many today would say that they have no interest in metaphysical questions and are wholly unconscious of any experience which could be called 'religious'. We cannot detect the inner heart and mind of those who are inarticulate; it may be that those of the modern world who are enmeshed in the turmoil of urban life, or who have enjoyed only a practical, scientific education, are rarely or even never aware of any glimmerings of a Beyond. But what we may call the spiritual life of humanity as manifested in painting, music, sculpture, architecture, poetry and religion, not to mention heroic virtue, is as much in need of explanation as are man's astonishing technological achievements.

Man cannot explain himself, but he should not try to explain himself away. Science, given sufficient data, can show that at a certain point in the story of our planet life appeared, but Science cannot explain why that particular concatenation of circumstances should have produced a living thing. This life is a new thing in the planet's history. Conceivably the production of life might be the explanation of the preceding agelong process, but certainly the process does not explain that which issued from it. If—to be absurd for a moment—we could imagine an amoeba saying to itself, 'I feel within me strange, hitherto unimagined powers and hopes and intimations, but of course I am in reality only a collocation of whirling electrons, and my sentient life is but a phantasy', we should, I think, have a parallel to those who would derive man's technological faculties from his animal inheritance, but would explain away all his spiritual sensitivities as insubstantial self-deceptions. Man is a new thing in the planet's history, and the new thing about him is not his technological ability, for many animals and insects are wonderful technicians. The new, inexplicable and altogether marvellous thing about him is that grace which in the mathematician traces the patterns of the universe, in the artist declares its beauty, in the philosopher seeks to apprehend it as a whole, and in the man of religion feels after that which is beyond. Well might St Augustine cry out, 'What therefore am I, O my God? What is my human nature?'

The animals take the world as they find it, and do not rail at fate or fortune or frustration. The unsatisfied animal is man, nor will his heart be satisfied by anything the universe can offer. His curiosity is insatiable or infinite. If Science could discover all her secrets and close her book of knowledge, man would still have questions. Man endlessly seeks that good wherein his happiness would lie, but his desire for that good is boundless, and the peace of perfect happiness for which he craves lies always out of reach. The animals are aware, no doubt, of change, but they have no tragic sense of the transience of all things earthly; their days are not shadowed by the conscious imminence of death; they have no sense of the imperfection of all things, for the notion of perfection is not theirs; they are aware of limitation, but they do not cry out for the infinite. If many men still live in these respects 'like the beasts that perish', they fail to illustrate that which is most singular and new and distinctive in man's nature. The longing for the infinite is set in the heart of man.

Scientists might 'explain' this longing for the infinite in terms of glands or some other bodily disturbances, but that is no more an explanation than the 'explanation' of life in terms of molecules. There is a very old saying, 'Nature does nought in vain.' Fish are furnished with fins because there is the ocean for their swimming; birds have developed wings because there is the air in which to fly. It would be strange and paradoxical if there were nothing, nothing at all, to answer the visions or correspond with the yearnings of the poets, artists, seers and prophets of mankind. 'The soul is born for the perceiving of an infinite good, which is God,' said St Bonaventure, 'wherefore in him alone should it rest and him enjoy.'

Infinite and eternal are in this sense negative terms in that they point to the indefinable and unimaginable beyond the reach of space or lapse of time. It has been the confident conviction of many of the most sensitive of mankind, not merely of so-called religious men, that in some way they have, at least at moments, been in mysterious touch with that which is beyond. Traherne could cry out, 'We see the seeds of Eternity sparkling in our natures.' No animal, we think, can feel like that, and even if in fact we are not so far elevated above the skylarks as we suppose, there remains the mystifying fact that man has a sense of the perfect, the eternal and the infinite.

So far at least as Evolution has hitherto developed, 'Life's great diapason ends in man'. We cannot explain man, or at least that which is most significant about him, in terms of protons and electrons or even of the animals. Man, said Goethe, is 'the first conversation which Nature has with God'. But about God, a name for the Power behind phenomena, can man know anything?

3

LIFE IS RESPONSE

FOR us, as for all animals, life is response to our environment. Even when we are in deep sleep, we respond to our environment by breathing. When all response ceases, we are dead. When the first living creatures emerged from the slime to become fish, animals or birds, they learnt gradually to adapt themselves to their new environment, the ocean, the dry land, the air. What, then, is man's environment? Charles Kingsley wrote a hymn or poem for boys beginning:

> God, who created me
> Nimble and light of limb
> In three elements free,
> To run, to ride, to swim . . .

but this is an inadequate analysis. We respond, of course, to our physical environment. Faced by a brick wall, we can avoid it or knock it down or, if we be young enough, vault over it; in one way or another we must respond to it. We respond even to the remotest stars visible in the sky either by turning our attention from them or by observing them with wonder.

But even the animals and insects, or some of them, respond to more than a merely physical environment. The construction of an ant-hill, the ordered wheeling of a flock of birds, the complicated communal and co-operative life of bees are indications of some psychic continuum or essential psychic relationship which is not purely physical or, as we say, material.

Animals and even insects, then, are aware of one another,

but man is, or he may be, aware of his fellow as a person. I catch the eye of many as I walk along the street. They respond to my glance in differing ways. To some, as I can see, I am a thing, an obstacle to be avoided, a human being, no doubt, but nothing at all to them. Others return my glance in a friendly or human way, and perhaps we say 'Good morning'. Sometimes, as I pass a man, though we exchange the most fleeting glance, yet clearly without words he answers me; we shall never meet again or speak together, but in that brief moment by a mysterious interchange of recognition we have signalled to one another as in some way kindred spirits.

Such chance meeting falls far short of friendship which is a deeper and more intimate mutual knowledge of one another in two persons. But what is it to know persons? In a remarkable passage at the beginning of his book *Between Man and Man*, Martin Buber describes a dream that has often come to him. At first some violent incident occurs; then he utters a cry 'inarticulate but in strict rhythm, rising and falling, swelling to a fulness which my throat could not endure were I awake, long and slow, quiet, quite slow and very long, a cry that is a song'. Then from a distance there comes an answering cry as if some question had been asked and was being answered. Finally there comes to him a quiet certitude that something, not to be defined, has happened. Meeting a person, when at any deep level we meet a person, is like that: something in us cries out and meets with a response. The faces and clothes of the people we meet are an element in our physical environment, but friendship indicates a spiritual or non-physical environment. We are aware of persons as surely as we are aware of things.

We are here outside the sphere of Science. There are, indeed, several sciences which deal with man, psychology, sociology, politics and ethics; but Science has to deal with general 'laws', with averages, with abstract principles. These sciences may help us better to understand our friends, but they cannot enter the private world of friendship. Yet it is important for my present argument that my friend, known as a friend, is at least as real and objective an element in my experience as is the brick wall facing me. Indeed, as regards the wall, the physicists have made me a little uncomfortable or uncertain in respect of its solidity and objectivity; of the reality of my friend as a person I have no doubts at all. I am aware, in fact, of a personal environment as well as of an environment of things, and to both of these, the latter physical, the former psychic, spiritual or at least non-physical, I make response.

I venture here upon a short digression the significance of which will later, I hope, appear. Very familiar is the old philosophic tag, 'I think; therefore I am', but I have learnt, particularly from Professor John MacMurray, how unsatisfactory is that argument. I think, but how can I jump from my thinking to a conviction of the reality of the things or persons of which I think? 'You are only part of my dream', said the Red Queen to Alice. I suspect that many people making no claim to be philosophers have looked into the abyss of solipsism, as it is called, the nightmare that we are only dreaming everything. The fact is, we do not know ourselves at all except in relation to things and other people (and perhaps to God). A little child only becomes conscious of itself as an individual very gradually, and always in relation to its mother and perhaps to brothers and sisters and to the surroundings of the nursery. Enough, however, for my immediate purposes that we know persons, as persons, to be part of our environment, and in knowing others we know ourselves.

What occurs when at a picture-gallery I stand and gaze

upon some picture or sit listening to a composition by Mozart at a concert? In the one case light-waves, as they are called, in the other sound-waves strike upon my senses. As a result of this, by a process or alchemy which is beyond our understanding, I see the picture, and I hear the music. Science has much to tell me, if I have the patience to listen, about the structure of the canvas, the composition of the pigments or about the violin-strings and the vibrations of the notes; but I am seeing a picture or hearing music, an experience which is beyond the touch of Science. If I can persuade an artist to discourse to me about the picture, or a musician about the music, my appreciation will be deepened, and because all men differ from each other, no two men have precisely the same experience as they look or listen. Titian or Mozart speaks a different word to each; yet it is they who speak, and my experience of the picture or the music, whether it be intended or not, is in some way a personal communication from the artist to myself. Beauty imparted through painter or musician is part of my spiritual or non-physical environment.

What ought we to say, then, of Beauty in the natural order? Let me take as an example a sunset on a quiet evening. I recollect one such sunset in particular:

> Far off the eastern shores of Newfoundland
>   We watch the fiery descent of day—
> The azure sky above, beneath, a strand
>   Of amethyst; then golden light, then grey
>   Melting within the tranquil waves, but they
> A soft, empurpled vintage breathe and glow:
>   Grass-green round rusty prow ripples the spray.
> In sky and sea these speechless glories show
> The image of His mind, His seal, who made them so.

Is this conclusion really justified?

What really happened when I saw that sunset? What was really there? If I had been able to fly up to the clouds, I should not have found the colours which I saw from the ship's deck, nor would the water have appeared green had I jumped over the ship's side to look more closely. Light-waves striking upon the retina of my eye and provoking electric currents to my brain were interpreted as these colours by my mind. If I enquire further about these light-waves and electric currents I am told of molecules and protons, neutrons, electrons and photons, themselves un-coloured, which merely make the sunset as I saw it more mysterious. The sunset 'spoke to me', as we say, in the same way as Titian or Mozart speaks to me. It seems, therefore, most natural or even inevitable to suppose that through the sunset, as I see it, I receive a communication from that Power or Being which or who is the Author and Ground of these protons and electrons. We may prefer to call that Power Matter or Nature; but 'Matter' seems to me a peculiarly bad word here with all the wrong connota-tions; and 'Nature' suggests a process rather than a com-municant. The natural word, I think, is God. But what-ever name be used, we all, atheists and theists, are aware that Beauty in nature speaks to us. Here is another element in our human environment which eludes the reach of Science.

I have said that Titian and Mozart speak to us, but I certainly cannot tell you what they say! This personal communication of himself by the artist is non-propositional; it cannot be defined in sentences. It is true that any man may attempt to state in stumbling words what Titian or what Mozart 'means to me', but the words will fall far short of the experience and can never convey the experience itself to any other person. When I speak of the apprehen-sion of Beauty in Nature as in some mysterious way a personal communication from that Power which is the Beyond of all our sensible experience, I am not suggesting that something is said which can be set down in words and sentences.

It may be objected that it is of 'mere feelings' that I am writing now, and that in mere feelings there is neither validity nor truth. But can there be 'mere' feeling? If I feel, I must feel something. Toothache is not 'mere feeling'; it is response, it may be to an abscess in the mouth. My feeling of delight in the painting or the music is my response, my right or, it may be, my wrong, response to Titian or Mozart. The delight, the wonder and the thankfulness with which I look upon the sunset is my response, my right or wrong response, to that Power or Being which is Beyond, and for which my name is God.

The apprehension of Beauty, it may be said, is a very private and personal experience, but I call it part of our environment because it comes to us from without, through the work of artists or through Nature. It is not of our contrivance. I come now to an equally private and personal experience, our sense of duty and of obligation. The Marxists maintain, as I understand them, that all our ethical ideas, our notions of right and wrong, are nothing but a reflection of the social conditions of the time, the moral ideas of any generation being no more than the prejudices of the ruling class adopted and imposed for their own advantage. There is truth in this, for much morality is a matter of convention, but not all. Though he disguised his moral indignation under cover of scientific terminology, it was in response to the call of a higher and more lasting Justice that Karl Marx repudiated the 'bourgeois morality' of his day.

Men differ widely from age to age, and even from country to country, in their ideas of what is right and wrong, but amongst civilized people and between those recognized as the great teachers of mankind, such as Confucius, the Buddha, Plato and the Christ, there is a large measure of ethical agreement. This must be ascribed to ethical insight, not, as the Marxist theory would demand, to similar conditions of production.

This sense of obligation, of 'ought', of what Kant called 'the categorical imperative', is most mysterious. If I know anything at all, I know that I ought to be gentle, not cruel, that I ought to be patient, not irritable, that I ought to have good will towards all and to none bear malice. If anywhere we have certitude, assurance, knowledge, it is here. It is true that not all men everywhere will recognize these principles, but as man has become more humane, that is, more truly human, his insight into moral truth has grown. Perhaps I should write of moral imperatives rather than moral truth. Be that as it may, we must not impose upon reality any theories which deny our deepest intuitions, the surest knowledge of our hearts.

Let me take an historical example. Centuries before Jesus, Socrates declared that it is better to suffer evil than to do it. He may be said to have died for this conviction. How did Socrates know this? It is quite certain that he could not have learnt it from any study of Nature, for no such principle is known to the Nature considered by the biologists. He cannot have learnt it from a study of history, partly because he did not study history, and partly because history might as well be claimed to suggest the opposite. Socrates himself ascribed his assurance to a mysterious Voice within. Here, then, is a principle which we also, I take it, recognize as true and as of binding obligation, and which we accept not because Socrates enunciated it but in response to our own insight. It comes to us as a Voice from beyond this world of confusion and of compromise.

47

It seems to be a unique power of man that he is capable of reverence or has a sense of the sacred. This is part of the mystery of man's awareness of the infinite. Truth, Goodness, Beauty he regards, if he be a civilized man, as of absolute or unqualified worth; the demands of conscience are to him of absolute or unconditional obligation. It will not do to say that these notions are the conventions of the period, the class, the social conditions of our upbringing. They are the profound intuitions and certainties of man as he grows from barbarism into the fuller realization of human nature.

This sense of reverence, of the sacred, belongs to man as man. The savage may regard as of infinite worth some wretched fetish, a thing of sticks and straw and bones; he that we regard as childish. Indeed, the story of the growth may regard as of binding obligation some rule of taboo of civilization or of the gradual development of man into the stature of full humanity can be told in terms of his gradual appreciation of what is really of absolute worth and is really of unconditional obligation. But here in this world of the relative, the imperfect, the qualified we touch the absolute, the unqualified, the unconditioned. We are in touch with the Beyond.

Alfred Sadd was a missionary working in the Pacific Islands who in the last war was captured by the Japanese. They spread a Union Jack before him on the ground and bade him spit upon it. Picking it up, instead, he kissed it, and they shot him then and there. Was his action sensible or prudent? Who would raise that question? We read sometimes that the Victoria Cross has been awarded posthumously for some action of outstanding heroism. We do not ask whether the soldier acted foolishly. Self-preservation may be one of the strongest instincts in man, but he is an unhappy man who does not know that there rest upon

48

him obligations of loyalty, of love, of honour more important than the preservation of his life. Moral obligation is not less a part of our personal environment than is Beauty, though we have no physical organ like the eye through which its admonitions come to us.

> Stern daughter of the voice of God!
> O Duty! if that name thou love
> Who art a light to guide, a rod
> To check the erring and reprove.

Duty, it may be, is a less lovely name than loyalty, but my point is clear that through moral obligation we are in touch with the infinite, the unconditioned, which religious men call God.

But we must be careful here. It has been customary among religious people to speak of conscience as 'the voice of God'. All manner of cruelties and iniquities have been perpetrated in the name of conscience which may be but the voice of convention or even an idealizing of unconscious motives. Our duty is to cultivate an instructed, sensitive and tender conscience, receptive of new light. As through manifold generations men supposed that the sun revolves round the earth, and only in comparative recent times have they learnt the truth of the revolutions of the planets round the sun, so through unnumbered generations they supposed that they should love their fellow-tribesmen, regarding all other men as enemies, and only in relatively recent times have come to a deeper understanding. In both cases we only gradually approximate to truth, but it is to truth in both cases that we approximate. There is no justification for regarding astronomical discoveries as reliable while we treat ethical insight as 'mere feeling'. In both cases, though in very different ways, we are learning of that Power which moves the universe. Two points I am here seeking to sub-

stantiate, first, that the spiritual or non-physical realm of obligation is quite as real and 'objective' a part of our environment as is the physical, and, second, that while the content
of what we think we ought to do is often given us through
convention, in the last resort this mysterious sense of *ought*
comes to us as a Voice from beyond this passing world.

Life is response to our environment. I have argued in
this chapter that the physical or material is only part of our
environment. We are quite as clearly and certainly aware
of persons as we are of things; we have no ground in our
experience which should lead us to judge that solidity is
'real' while beauty is 'unreal'; so the moral like the beautiful
is part of our spiritual or non-material environment. We
must here agree with Teilhard de Chardin, as Karl Stern
interprets him,[1] that 'there exist two methods by which we
can approach the phenomena of nature: the poetic-intuitive
and the scientific-analytic, and that they are of equal
validity, each on its own plane, but not of equal applica-
bility. Then we realize that the scientific-analytic method,
with its breath-taking results, cannot possibly be applied
to a great number of questions, such as the mystery of
creation, the infinite variety of living forms, the destiny of
man, the presence of hate and corruption and their co-
existence, in the same world, with love and beauty.' It
seems to me that, if we deny this, we are not being honest,
we are imposing our theories upon reality, we are not
allowing reality to speak to us. Day-to-day life is response
to people and to things, but we are all aware, at least from
time to time, of the unconditioned, the unqualified, the
absolute or infinite. Religion is conscious response to this
Infinite or Unconditioned apprehended as the Great Spirit
or as God. To religion, therefore, I now turn.

[1] *The World of Teilhard*, ed. R. T. Francoeur (Helicon Press,
Baltimore, 1961), p. 44.

4

RELIGION

HAD it been possible, I should have liked up to this point to avoid the use of the term 'God', which both for religious people and those who think themselves irreligious carries associations improper to my argument so far. We are aware of a universe, an unimaginable complex of patterns, not a chaos; we recognize in the structure of this universe the marks of what we must call a Reason corresponding to the reason in man; of this the mathematicians produce sufficient evidence. Unimaginable Power and inscrutable Intelligence mark the whole which, the further we probe it through molecular physics, becomes ever more mysterious and even immaterial. We recognize a vast Process which we call Evolution and which, especially as we can observe it in animate nature, is informed by an immanent Purpose or Intelligence. So far, I think, there should be agreement between atheists and theists. Religion, I think, only arises whereby some quickening illumination or ecstasy of the spirit man addresses this mysterious Power as 'Thou', or, in the modern idiom, as 'You'.

Sometimes on a journey over difficult country one comes to a chasm over which it is needful for the traveller to jump. In the course of a logical argument such jumps are not permissible. I will admit therefore that at this point I make no claim that one is compelled in logic to move from a recognition of the rational order of the universe to an attitude of worship. It is one thing to recognize Power,

51

Order, Beauty in the world around us; it is another to cry out in wonder and in adoration 'It is Thou! It is Thou!' One can either halt in the beauty of the creature, says St Bonaventure, or move beyond.

I make here no claim to inescapable pressure of logic. Yet my argument is logical. We are compelled to recognize Power and Intelligence in the world as reviewed by Science. Power, indeed, may be quite impersonal, but intelligence is personal, for we cannot sensibly call a mere thing intelligent. Theologians should not immediately leap to the happy conclusion that behind phenomena we apprehend a Person, for a person means to us a being with the qualities that distinguish humanity from the beasts. But if we may say that terms must be either abstract or impersonal or personal, it may be agreed that the Intelligence which we recognize in the natural order is not an abstraction; it cannot be impersonal as if it were a thing; we must therefore call it personal, however inadequate that may be.

But we may go a little further. I have spoken of a work of art, whether it be a poem or a painting or a musical composition, as a personal communication from the artist to ourselves. It will, then, be natural if not inevitable to regard the beauty which we apprehend in Nature or through Nature as a personal communication from that which is Beyond, and which cannot be regarded as impersonal. I conceive that this sense of a Presence is common at least occasionally to all men of sensitive spirit before the mysteries and beauties of the changing seasons or the silence of the snow-clad mountains or the pleasant fields and rivers of our own countryside. We must not try to define the Presence, but it is not impersonal.

Again, we are aware of the voice of conscience, of the call of duty, of the demands of loyalty, the obligations of affection. No doubt our language is inadequate and metaphorical; we are, however, as I think, shut up to personal terms, such as voice, call, demand and obligation. This 'categorical imperative' within us, this sense of a moral obligation which is absolute and unconditional, is to us as a personal communication upon our response to which our honour, our quality, our worth depend. Self-preservation is one of the strongest of the human instincts, but obedience to duty must be set before self-preservation. This conviction comes to us as a Voice from beyond this world of space and change. I must call it a personal communication.

Finally, man is touched from time to time with a sense of the infinite and the eternal, perhaps when he falls in love, when he looks upon his first-born child, at a sad graveside, when he is faced with an irrevocable decision or reads of some act of heroic virtue. This sense for the infinite and the eternal is set in our hearts and is not to be distinguished from that Presence of which at any time or on any occasion we may be suddenly aware.

I judge, therefore, that all men are aware of God, but many do not realize that it is of God that they are aware. I may revert here to Martin Buber's dream to which I earlier referred. He utters a long cry, then comes a mysterious answering cry, and he knows in his dream that something has happened, something has been accomplished. There is religion where in the midst of the mysteries of Nature, of life, of death, and under a strange sense of the Presence, man cries 'Thou!' and hears an answering 'thou!'

Can we be sure, however, that the religion we have, or wish we had, is not mere self-deception, 'wish-fulfilment', superstition? We look for some logical proof or external guarantee that our religious consciousness corresponds to some reality—and we look in vain. 'If you ask God for a positive guarantee that he is good, which you can file securely along with your Birth Certificate,' said Dr W. A. L. Elmslie, 'the document is not forthcoming.' We are troubled by this partly because we tend to distrust the flickerings of religion within ourselves, and partly because it has become customary to contrast the subjectivity of faith with the objectivity of scientific knowledge. Wordsworth felt

> A presence that disturbs me with the joy
> Of elevated thoughts; a sense sublime
> Of something far more deeply interfused,
> Whose dwelling is the light of setting suns,
> And the round ocean and the living air,
> And the blue sky, and in the mind of man.

There is a passage to much the same effect in Virgil. Have we here the expression of an experience which is 'just mere feeling', as we say, due, it may be, to mood or temperament or fine weather or a good digestion, or is it, perhaps, an insight into some reality?

This issue, so significant for our outlook upon life and upon the world, is not a scientific question, nor is it a philosophical question if we mean by philosophy mere thinking. It is a question of feeling, but this does not render it irrational. In a famous chapter of his book *Statement and Inference* the distinguished logician J. Cook Wilson pointed out that in gratitude and reverence, as in aesthetic and moral judgments, Reason 'can only express itself emotionally'. Where we cannot investigate in any scientific way, there right feeling leading to a right response is the only pathway to reality. A happy home is a reality, though it elude the instruments of scientific investigation and be known by feeling only. All appreciation of beauty is by feeling, but it is an appreciation of a reality that is given and is not 'mere' feeling. We may not rule out Wordsworth's

sense of a disturbing Presence simply on the ground that
this Presence is not to be verified by any experiment or test
devised by Science. Feeling in these matters is response; is
it a valid or a misconceived response? Is he who feels with
Wordsworth self-deceived, or is there a reality or truth
which he dimly apprehends? Science is mute on such a
theme, but such questions, neither meaningless nor foolish,
rise inevitably in the mind of a sensitive spirit in the
presence of natural beauty or sublimity. Thus Coleridge, for
instance, addresses the great mountain above Chamonix:

> Thou first and chief, sole sovereign of the Vale!
> O struggling with the darkness all the night,
> And visited all night by troops of stars,
> Or when they climb the sky or when they sink:
> Companion of the morning-star at dawn,
> Thyself Earth's rosy star, and of the dawn
> Co-herald: wake, O wake, and utter praise!
> Who sank thy sunless pillars deep in Earth?
> Who fill'd thy countenance with rosy light?
> Who made thee parent of perpetual streams?

These questions would have been answered in early mytho-
logies by the naming of many gods and goddesses whom
Science has since made incredible, but there is nothing
either scientific or unscientific about the poet's own reply:

> Thou kingly Spirit throned among the hills,
> Thou dread ambassador from Earth to Heaven,
> Great hierarch! tell thou the silent sky,
> And tell the stars, and tell yon rising sun
> Earth, with her thousand voices, praises GOD.

Shelley, like Coleridge, wrote of the impression made

upon him by Mont Blanc ('stupendous mountain', as Coleridge called it):

> Thou hast a voice, great mountain, to repeal
> Large codes of fraud and woe; not understood
> By all, but which the wise, and great, and good
> Interpret, or make felt, or deeply feel.

I am citing here, it may be said, from imaginative literature, and imagination is no guide to reality. It is true that unbridled imagination can conjure up all manner of absurdities and unrealities, but imagination, it may be, is our sole guide to truth. Certainly it is by a gift and exercise of inspired imagination that the scientist makes his great discoveries. It is true that the splendid imagination of great scientists can be tested and confirmed by physical experiments as the imaginations of poets and of seers and prophets cannot be, but it would be unjustifiable and foolish to assume that only the imaginations of the scientists can point to truth. The poet or the prophet speaks without any authority but that of the words that come from him, but he tells us what he sees, not merely what he feels. If poet or prophet speak of a Presence where the scientist must speak only of a Power or an Intelligence, it would be very presumptuous to suppose that because poet and prophet cannot prove their contentions by experiment, they are therefore talking nonsense. Moreover, there is something in all men of any spiritual sensitivity, not least in scientists, which responds to what the poets say, however mysterious it be, and however little our apprehension can be put into dogmatic statements.

In this connection it is well to remember that science no less than religion rests upon a faith. While men believed that the outbreak of thunder and lightning, the sudden rising of the storm at sea, the revolution of the crops from

56

the death of winter to the birthtime of spring and to the fruition of harvest, were due to the unpredictable and often discordant whims of Zeus, Poseidon and Demeter, there could be no Science. The scientist assumes (that is, it is with him a matter of faith) that the world he is studying is a rational order, and that a rational account is to be found for every event which may occur. He studies a system of uniformities, as he supposes, not of whimsies. In this assumption of faith he has been amply justified. In the course of his researches he may have to alter or abandon old and cherished theories, but on the basis of this assumption of what I may call the trustworthiness of Nature's operations he grows in knowledge step by step.

So by imaginative insight, step by step, we grow in knowledge of that spiritual or super-sensible or non-physical environment which, through the physical, surrounds us at all times. In this sphere, too, I am sure it is right to speak of *knowledge*. For instance, I am confident that the scientist in his heart (which means when he is not merely rationalizing but thinking with the whole force of his personality) is much more certain that he ought not to be cruel and bad-tempered than he is certain of any of the physical theories in his learned text-books. We rightly speak of scientific knowledge, and stand in awe before it, but it is not the only kind of knowledge we have to guide us through the tangled ways of life. True, our knowledge of the world of the spirit lags far behind our knowledge of the material world, but that, I suppose, is not surprising, for the physical world is the environment man shares with the animal creation, whereas the spiritual is that new environment to which he must learn gradually and painfully to adapt himself.

But such knowledge as we have about spiritual things, it may be said, is knowledge about life. Can we have knowledge of that Being, that Presence, that Infinite, that Power and Intelligence of which the poets speak and to which the study of physical Nature itself points?

I have, I hope, made plain what I am meaning by this word 'God'. The Being of God cannot be defined; it cannot be pictured or imagined or conceived by the mind of man, but if that were a reason for supposing that God is not Reality, we ought also to say, as we do not, that electricity is no reality. We know what electricity will do; electricity itself cannot be pictured or imagined or conceived. When I speak of God, I am meaning that Power and Intelligence which Science apprehends through Nature, that Infinite which hovers over us and touches us in the sublime, the beautiful, the immeasurably lovable, that Voice which as from another world speaks to our hearts with wordless and unconditional authority, that Presence of which from time to time we are aware, and which because it is mysteriously personal we are constrained to address as 'Thou'.

Can we know anything about God? We have answered the question in part by the statement of what we mean by God. That infinite Presence recognized through all glories and sublimities of Nature, in all boundless human love, in the inexorable demands of duty and of loyalty, is known in some degree through the modes and instruments whereby we become aware of it. Religion is response to God. True religion will be the right response to God in that environment in which our lives are set.

Here I lay stress upon environment. There is a mysticism, found in many religions, which claims an unmediated, direct contact with the Divine, an absorption of the individual in the One, the All. Years ago in Mysore I was taken to hear the court musician play upon his stringed instrument, rather like a great guitar, the name of which I have forgotten. With his left hand in the treble he played all manner of trills and runs and intricate figures, using semi-tones and demi-semi-tones. This fairy virtuoso performance is said to represent the phantasmagoria of the motions, colours, sounds and scents of the multifarious and variegated existence of our consciousness. With his right hand in the bass he sustained one steady, unchanging thrum, analogue of the underlying Unity, the Unchanging, the unconscious consciousness of Brahma. The mood expressed and induced by such music is not wholly unfamiliar. By what may be an exercise of auto-hypnotism through the deliberate emptying of the mind, the suppression of all desiring and all willing, aided, it may be, by a technical control of breathing as in Yoga, it is possible, at least for the adept, to sink back through all the differentiations of persons and of things into an undifferentiated unity in which the self is absorbed and taken up into the All, the One. The reality of this mystical experience we need not question; whether it should be called religious experience is another matter. If it be through our finite environment that we become aware of the infinite Beyond, through the experiences of life that we become aware of God, it would not seem likely that we shall attain to truth by suppressing or denying our environment. True religion, then, I shall take to be the right response to God in that environment in which our lives are set.

But what is the relation of 'true religion', as I have called it, to the many religions with which the world abounds? What is the right response of man to God? Hinduism and Buddhism, Judaism, Jainism, Islam, Christianity offer differing answers; is one more likely than another? Has life any meaning of which we can be sure? Has man a hope and calling beyond these passing years, or is he destined for the dustbin all too soon?

True religion or the right relation between man and God

will be the religion for the whole human race. We have reached what we call the technocratic age. The vast sky-scraping oblong erections which adorn or disfigure all the proud cities of five continents are a symbol of that common technocratic civilization which is becoming and must become world-wide. A common civilization can neither cohere nor enjoy stability apart from some common faith, the acceptance of common ideals and standards underlying the pleasing and significant varieties of race and nation. The peace and prosperity of a world-civilization presuppose a world-religion. None of the 'world-religions', as they are at present, is adapted to the needs of the whole human family or to serve as the foundation of a world-society. All the great religions of mankind have produced their saints who, I suspect, recognize one another across all barriers. I do not know what an 'ideal' Christianity or Judaism or Islam or Buddhism or Hinduism might be; it will here be sufficient if I make the point that 'Christianity', by which I mean the organization of the churches and the conventional Christian ethical and theological ideas, is not adapted to the needs and necessary outlook of man in this scientific age.

There is a remark of St Augustine which has, I have no doubt, caused much disquiet in the minds of orthodox theologians. 'That very thing', he says in his *Retractations*, 'which is now called the Christian religion existed in antiquity nor was absent since the beginning of the human race until such time as the Christ should come in the flesh, whence true religion,[1] which existed already, began to be called Christianity'.

Clearly St Augustine did not mean that all religions are the same, he had plenty to say against the paganisms of his

[1] Or 'The true religion' or 'real religion' (*vera religio, Retractationes* I, 13.3).

60

day. Nor could he have meant by 'Christian religion' simply the Christian Church, for this has certainly not existed since the beginning of the human race. What he meant, I think, was this: there has always been a Word of God to man; it is the capacity to hear that Word and to respond to it which is man's peculiar dower. In wonder and in beauty, in the imperious claims of truth, in the demands and obligations of love and loyalty and duty man has from the beginning heard, however dimly, and responded, however imperfectly, in awe and by obedience or thankfulness; this Word of God, the will of God for man, the mind of God for man, was at last enmanned or incarnated in the Person of Christ; Christian religion or the religion of Christ is therefore true religion.

This is not at all the same thing as to say that 'Christianity' is the true religion and all others are false. From the beginning of the world in all ages and in all religions, as I understand St Augustine, there have been men who have been aware of God; their insight may have been limited, as indeed is our own, but according to the light given them their response was in reverence, obedience and thankfulness. It was the Christ who heard clearly where others had heard confusedly, and who responded rightly where they had responded fumblingly. This, at least, is very much what I want to say, but let me come at it in my own way.

It is difficult to come at it because on the way there are two thick and prickly jungles which I must traverse. The real Jesus is to most within and without the churches almost invisible because of the theological trappings which now surround his figure. Second, when that difficulty is out of the way, there remains an historical question of extreme complexity. I must leave till the next chapter the consideration of this second barrier.

Everybody knows that Christian dogma declares Jesus

Christ to be Very God and Very Man. I hope that before I finish I shall make clear the religious insight upon which this dogma rests. The statement is intelligible and natural *in terms of the philosophical ideas when it was promulgated long ago.* Today to speak of a person as being both God and man is not paradox, it is nonsense. When I was young it was customary to say that Jesus did some things as man and some things as God. It is, I judge, absolutely impossible to make that really intelligible to ourselves today. The doctrine of the 'divinity' of Jesus Christ, as popularly understood by Christians and non-Christians alike, is taken to mean that he was God but was somehow a man or at least God under human conditions. In fact he is taken for an unreal person, a kind of being with whom historians cannot deal at all, for historians can only treat of men. Nor am I dealing only with a popular misconception, for the orthodox classical doctrine of Christ's person is that in him God became man but not *a* man; we, to use theological language, are created and fallen spirits incarnate; that is what it means to be a man; he was the uncreated Second Person of the Trinity incarnate; therefore he was not *a* man.

Such language, not the insight behind it but the language itself, is today incredible or meaningless. Jesus Christ was a real human person, an historical figure. God is spoken of in the New Testament as 'the God and Father of our Lord Jesus Christ', the God and not the Father only. Jesus walked by faith in God, he nourished his life by prayer to God, and his course was directed by obedience to God. If we continue to speak of the 'divinity' of Christ (as we well may), our thought must not be inconsistent with the plain fact that he was a man who lived in faith, in prayer and in obedience. However unlike us, he was a real human being. I insist upon this for two reasons, first that the idea of a person who is half God and half man or wholly God and wholly man makes no sense today; it belong to the world of mythology and not of history. Second, those among whom he moved in Judaea and Galilee expressed very different judgments about him. Some thought he was a prophet. Some wondered if he might be Elijah come to life again (and here I like Dr George Caird's very proper observation that there must have been a mighty vein of granite in him if he could be mistaken for Elijah). Some wanted 'to make him king', that is, they took him, or wanted to take him, for the political Messiah of the Jewish hope. Some wondered if he might be the expected 'Coming One', and others apparently said 'he has a devil'. But none of his contemporaries according to the available evidence ever doubted that he was a real man.

But, granted that, what do we really know about him?

5

THE HISTORICAL QUESTION

I SHOULD first explain why I regard this matter as so vitally important, and why I give so much of my space to Jesus the Christ. History reveals many great religious figures such as the Buddha, Jeremiah, Zoroaster, Plato, Plotinus and many others; from these we can learn much to our advantage. I have insisted above that Jesus of Nazareth was a real historical, human being; I recognize as incredible to us or unintelligible to us much of the language used about him in the traditional theories of his person; but I believe that these obscure and remote attempts to represent his significance are pointing toward the truth, that his coming is as epoch-making, as new, as wonderful as these theories presuppose. We are beginning to find a language suited and intelligible to the present time.

There must have been a moment in unimaginably far distant time when the star-dust or cosmic gases (or whatever be the proper term for first beginnings) began to cohere into the solid masses from which our planet with its rocks and seas was to be formed. After a lapse of immeasurable years there first appears life on earth, and a new and wonderful chapter has begun. Again after incalculable ages (but the length of time means nothing, for there was no one to measure it or think it long) appears man with his new, developing powers of speech and thought and reason, a being adapted to a new and spiritual environment of

wonder, of beauty, of moral obligation. Finally 'in the
fulness of time', to use the old phrase, there comes Jesus
the Christ, and I really believe, for reasons that I hope to
make more clear, that his coming marks a new epoch comparable in its significance to the coming of the preceding
epochs but with a new element of finality. Human history
is rightly divided into the two periods B.C. and A.D. Jesus
was a real man, not some semi-divine being, not one who
seemed to be man being really God *incognito*, but he was
the New Man, man at last rightly related to his fellows, to
Nature and to God.

Science, where it remains strictly Science, as I have
repeatedly said, is a-theist. The Intelligence which mathematicians, and the mental or conative impulse which
biologists, must recognize in the universal order or in the
course of Evolution, as we can trace it, is not in itself a
matter for direct scientific investigation. The scientist traces
what has happened; before the practical and technological
outcome of his researches we stand amazed. As a scientist
he does not speak of God, for as a scientist he is concerned
with phenomena, not with that new spiritual or non-
material, non-physical environment which is the prerogative
of man. But when man through his sense of wonder, of
beauty, of obligation, of love, of reverence, is touched with
the feeling of the Infinite, he must go on to relate that
Infinite to the 'matter' or 'Nature' from which he springs
and through which he is aware of the Beyond. To the religious man all the discoveries of Science must be welcome,
for, as the apostle Paul once said, 'all that is being made
manifest is light'. Evolution, our name for the universal
Process which Science explores, may be conceived as a
striving, an adventure, a groping, a 'guided groping', as de
Chardin calls it. It looks as if there were in the electrons
and molecules themselves some sort of embryonic, pre-

conscious consciousness instigating them to cohere with one another and to produce higher, more closely integrated forms. This *nisus* or tendency or innate striving is much more apparent in the sciences that deal with the development of life, of genera and species. In man at last this striving, this adventure becomes conscious; he deals consciously with his environment of things and people; in him the upward striving to that which is beyond strains towards the infinite. 'Matter' or 'Nature' has risen at last to respond to the infinite, however fitfully. 'Matter' which is 'energy' finds its fulfilment in personality which is 'spirit', for energy itself may be deemed embryonic spirit. 'The world is man: man in various stages of becoming'—so Fr Weigel summarizes de Chardin's central thought.[1] Matter is the matrix of spirit which is the upward striving universal energy.

Many years before Christ, Aristotle said that all motion and all change in the world, all the process of Evolution as we might put it, must be traced back ultimately to the Unmoved Mover whom we may call God. But how can that which does not move itself move anything else at all? The Unmoved Mover, says Aristotle, 'moves as an object of love'. An embryonic striving from within might be called an embryonic love. 'Matter' is moved by an embryonic striving for the infinite; it is in man that this striving becomes conscious. Man strives—how fitfully!—for union with that infinite of which he is aware through wonder, through reverence, through beauty, through the call of goodness and through love. It was in Jesus of Nazareth, as I believe, that the union with the infinite was at last achieved, who called God, Father.

But the initiative in the whole process comes from the Unmoved Mover, comes from God. We may as well say that the Creator draws as that the creature strives. The

[1] *The World of Teilhard*, p. 157.

mysterious energy which we call matter moves unconsciously or preconsciously towards man. Matter is the realm of time and space. Man, at least fitfully, through wonder, beauty and the sense of unconditioned obligation is in touch with the Infinite beyond time and space. When at last the Infinite is fully revealed, so far as man's grasp allows, and the Son answers to the Father, at that point an end of creation is reached, and the new era has begun for the human race.

Or let me put it in this way: from the point of view of the scientist as such the fact that Zoroaster, Jeremiah, Confucius and the Buddha emerged at about the same time in human history was due to an unpredictable and, so far as Science can tell, fortuitous mutation of genes. It is as legitimate or necessary for the philosopher or the theologian to say that at this point of history the Power evoked these figures. Thus the assertion of Christians that in the fulness of time 'God sent his Son' is not in any way incompatible with the assertion that Christ appeared in the course of the evolutionary process. All events have, as it were, an outside and an inside. The outside is the historical phenomenon which is the subject of scientific study; the inside is the relation of that event to the mysterious Power or Presence, which scientists must recognize but cannot study (because it is not a phenomenon), and which is the concern of philosophers, poets, theologians and seers.

But I must descend from these speculative heights to assured and sober history.

It is, I am told, a dogma widely promulgated by interested persons that Jesus Christ is the invention of the Christian imagination and, I suppose, of bourgeois self-interest. In historical enquiries it is well to be critical and, within reason, sceptical, but scepticism beyond a certain point is pathological, not scientific. Our knowledge of the historical existence of Jesus of Nazareth comes to us primarily, though not exclusively, from Christian sources. That there was such a person as Jesus, that he was executed by the Romans somewhere between AD 26 and 37 ('under Pontius Pilate'), that he became the accepted Founder of the religion soon called Christian, are facts to be accepted as assured. But what more do we know about him for certain? How far, in fact, can we trust the Gospels? Any modern reader of them finds puzzles or riddles in them and stories which strain the credulity of a scientific age. Scholars meticulously sifting and weighing every word tend to increase our perplexity and insecurity. Can we find firm ground on which to plant our feet?

The Gospels are inevitably suspect. First, they were avowedly written to awaken faith; second, their writers had very little idea of what we should call historical evidence, and, third, they are relatively late. If we count a generation as thirty years, we must admit that all our Gospels were written at least a generation after the death of Jesus; that leaves plenty of time for the distortion of fact, the growth of legend and the embellishments of faith. The Gospels differ among themselves; it is impossible to construct from them anything like a biography of Jesus or even a clear picture of the years of his public ministry; his sayings, even where they are correctly remembered, we have only in translation. It is substantially never possible for us to say of any recorded event 'that is exactly how it happened' or of any recorded saying 'that is precisely what he said'. The modern reader of the Gospels is attracted, puzzled, sceptical, uncertain. Where, if anywhere, can we be confident?

I would lay great stress and confidence upon any account of Jesus, whether direct or by implication, which can be derived from the one Christian writer who was certainly his contemporary, though perhaps his younger contemporary, the Apostle Paul. It is unlikely that Paul ever saw Jesus in the flesh, he gives us no stories of the ministry apart from the crucifixion, and he hardly ever directly quotes any saying of Jesus, so far as we can tell. He is thus up to a point a most disappointing and unsatisfactory witness. What little we can gather from him, however, is trustworthy. Paul was for a time the bitter enemy and persecutor of the young Christian movement; anything that could be said against Jesus by those who rejected him must have been well known to him. His 'conversion' implied his repudiation of the Pharisaic ideal in which he had been brought up and an acceptance of the new 'Way' which the Christians were declaring. Moreover, he tells us himself in one of his letters that not long after his conversion he went up to Jerusalem for the purpose of learning Peter's story (Gal. 1.18); Peter had been one of the closest companions of Jesus. Paul also knew James, the brother of Jesus, and others of the original Christian witnesses. Any historical evidence about Jesus, therefore, which we can derive from Paul is of first-class importance.

But how little evidence he appears to offer! He represents Christ, it may be said, as the Second Adam, the exalted Lord, the pre-existent Son of God, an altogether mythological and non-human, non-historical figure. Paul's flights of interpretation we must here disregard. He insists, however, in several places, as vital to his theology that Jesus was born a Jew (Rom. 9.5; Gal. 4.4), that he was believed to be of Davidic descent (Rom. 1.3), that he was a real man (Rom. 5.15, 19), that he worshipped God as his God and Father (Col. 1.3; Rom. 15.6; II Cor. 1.3; 11.31). This man Jesus, Paul tells us, was executed and buried (I Cor. 15.4); upon his death Paul insists repeatedly; he also says, a matter to which we must return, that after his death and burial he was seen alive by Peter, by the twelve apostles, by five hundred other witnesses, most of whom, Paul says, were still alive when he was writing; Jesus was later seen by James, then by 'all the apostles' and finally by Paul himself (I Cor. 15.5-8). We shall have to consider later whether these persons really saw him alive or only thought they saw him, but there seems to me quite unavoidable contemporary evidence that Jesus was a real man, brought up in Judaism, who died as a result of crucifixion at the hands of the Romans, and that after his death, though this is not at the moment relevant to my argument, a number of persons believed that he was alive again. Here, it seems to me, we are on quite sure historical ground.[1]

This is, perhaps, all the direct evidence we can draw from Paul, but, again, his indirect evidence is of first importance. He was brought up a Pharisee; as the leading persecutor of the infant church he was a fanatic for the Pharisaic outlook and way of life, for the meticulous keeping of the Law as the rabbis expounded and elongated it, for avoidance of contact with that which was 'unclean', for an unwillingness to share the blessings of God's rule with the 'uncircumcised dogs', the Greeks, the Romans, the barbarians. His conversion (however we 'explain' it psychologically or inter-

---

[1] The reader may ask whether it is quite certain that Paul really wrote the letters now ascribed to him. It is, I think, agreed amongst competent scholars that, apart from possible interpolations which do not concern the references given above, Paul certainly wrote Romans, Galatians, I and II Thessalonians, I and II Corinthians, Philippians, Philemon, most probably Colossians, possibly Ephesians and certainly not 'the epistle to the Hebrews'. The so-called 'pastoral epistles', I and II Timothy and Titus, almost certainly include authentic fragments of Pauline correspondence but are not in their present form of Pauline authorship. There is disagreement among scholars about some of the Pauline writings but not about the main epistles quoted above as certainly authentic.

70

pret it theologically) did not totally change his character; we can find traces of 'the old Adam', I think, in his correspondence. But from the moment of his conversion he was the devoted servant of Jesus Christ; as he himself says, 'five times I received the thirty-nine strokes at the hands of Jews; I was beaten three times by the Romans; once I was stoned; I was shipwrecked three times; I was adrift on the sea for a day and a night; I have endured many a perilous journey, being in dangers from rivers, from robbers, from the Jews, from the non-Jews, dangers in city and in the lonely country and on the sea and from false brethren; I have known toil and hardship, sleeplessness, hunger, thirst and starvation often; I have been cold and ill clad; and besides all that I have had to bear the burden of the care of all the churches' (II Cor. 11.24-28). There could be no doubt about his devotion, but his whole point of view had changed; the Pharisee whose life had been bounded and dignified by the Law now declared that the Law had been done away in a new dispensation; the Pharisee who at all costs had kept himself separate from the pagan world became the missionary who brought his gospel to the pagans of Asia Minor and of Europe and substituted for the old hard conception of legal righteousness the new law of love.

His writings, as a later New Testament writer properly observes, are often 'hard to understand' (II Peter 3.16), and many modern readers who are puzzled and offended by his obscure, Jewish and rabbinic forms of argumentation and theology fail to observe how complete and revolutionary was his conversion. That conversion of itself proves nothing; his theology is cast in forms that are often quite unthinkable by us today, but his immense importance for our immediate purpose is the indirect but clear and contemporary evidence he affords as to the kind of person Jesus

was. Not only is this shown in his abandoning an intro-
verted Judaism for a mission to all the world, but also in
his constant reiterated stress upon the duty of the Christian
to 'walk by the Spirit' and his very clear indication of what
will be the character of one who so walks by the Spirit. He
refers directly to the gentleness, the reasonableness, the
pitifulness, the love of Jesus; he who is possessed by the
Spirit, which, as he expressly states, is the Spirit of Jesus,
will be marked by hope and peace and joy and patience and
cheerfulness and helpfulness, by willingness to forgive, by
the love which is described in the familiar hymn of I
Corinthians 13.

Not only does Paul expressly say that this new spirit,
this new ethical ideal, this new type of life and experience
represents the Spirit of Jesus; we must believe him because
there is no other source whence it could be derived. To
suppose that he invented it is merely silly. We cannot suppose that a Pharisee while actually engaged in the persecution of a Church gathered round the name of Jesus suddenly
is seized in his own mind with a new ideal and new concept
of life not directly related to the faith that he was resisting,
and that he then ascribed his own discovery to the Jesus of
his enemies with whom henceforth he identified himself.
Besides this we have other evidence: the Gospels, later no
doubt than the Pauline epistles but demonstrably going
back to much earlier tradition, which confirm and indeed
explain what Paul says of the Spirit. My conclusion is that
though Paul rarely or never describes incidents in the life
of Jesus or quotes his words, he gives us a perfectly clear
and contemporary picture of the character of Jesus, the
kind of man he was. Our feet are on firm ground here.

We cannot date the Gospels with any certainty. The
scholars who contribute to the recent *Interpreter's Bible*
declare that probably Mark's Gospel is a compilation of

the oral tradition current in the Christian community at Rome in the sixties, and that Matthew is a revised and expanded edition of Mark written probably 'not far from the year 100', while Luke may probably be dated from the eighties or nineties of the first century. However, Matthew and Luke may be earlier. Dr G. B. Caird suggests that Luke collected and wrote down much of the material found in his Gospel 'perhaps during his two-year stay at Caesarea in AD 57-59, while Paul was in prison there' (Acts 24.27).[1] The Fourth Gospel raises its peculiar difficulties for the historian; it is probably to be dated towards the end of the first century, but 'the basic tradition on which the evangelist is working was shaped (it appears) in a Jewish-Christian environment still in touch with the synagogue, in Palestine, at a relatively early date, at any rate before the rebellion of AD 66'.[2]

The fascinating literary questions involved here are not for us. The Gospels were written at least a generation after the death of Jesus. It must be remembered, on the other hand, that one who had known and spoken with Jesus in youth might still be living in AD 100. Moreover, Luke expressly tells us that 'many' had undertaken to compile some sort of record before he wrote his Gospel; documents as well as oral tradition were, it seems, at his disposal.

Many years ago somewhere in South India I heard (without understanding a word) a local pastor preach to his congregation. The missionary who was with me told me that the preacher very earnestly, very sincerely and, as I should gather, very effectively was expounding some parable from the Gospels or some event in the life of Jesus. He retold the story as it was vividly present to his imagination, but in

[1] *St Luke* (Pelican Gospel Commentaries, 1963), p. 19.
[2] C. H. Dodd, *Historical Tradition in the Fourth Gospel* (Cambridge University Press, 1963), p. 426.

the retelling he had added much detail that was not in his original. The traditions of Jesus were at first entirely oral, and we must reckon with such embellishments and alterations in their verbal transmission before any were written down. Moreover, not only did the evangelists select from the pool of oral (and written) tradition that which in each case suited their particular purpose and interest, but we can even see here and there the adaptation of the tradition to different localities and to contemporary church problems. We can further note on occasion a heightening of the mysterious or marvellous in the supposed interests of piety. Sometimes the same saying appears in different contexts, sometimes we have apparently varying and seriously different accounts of the same event. The earth seems to quake beneath our feet. On the other hand, all our Gospels rest ultimately upon oral tradition and are not, after all, very far removed from the events which they narrate.

We may have substantial certainty, however, upon that which is essential. Quite certainly the evangelists did not consciously invent the stories which they told; and quite certainly they did not invent the figure who is central in all the stories. They had no idea of what we call scientific historical method and the testing of authorities; they had no idea of what we call the laws of nature, and they revelled in 'miracles'; but there must have been endless stories of Jesus endlessly retold, and the Gospels rest upon sober history. Where, then, can we be sure? Re-reading the Gospels in Greek at the age of seventy-seven, Dean Inge wrote: 'My impression is that there was a large authentic collection of the sayings of Christ, many of them far above the capacity of the evangelists to invent or even understand, and that the piecing together has been done with almost incredible clumsiness. The interpretations are mostly quite childish.'[1] That, I think, is the natural judgment of an open-minded scholar.

Let it be agreed that legendary, dogmatic and pious accretions have distorted the historical portrait given in the Gospels, and that rarely or never can our certainty be verbal. Often, however, we can have substantial certainty. Certainly when Mark wrote his Gospel, and almost certainly when the other evangelists compiled theirs, there were those still alive who had seen Jesus and a great many alive whose parents had seen and talked with him. There are, too, in the Gospels phrases used and situations described or assumed which cannot reasonably be regarded as the additions of piety or imagination. Above all, neither the evangelists nor folk-piety invented the figure of Jesus, who, as Peter says in Acts, 'went about doing good, for God was with him', and whose character is plainly if only implicitly described by Jesus' contemporary Paul. Paul says (I am quoting here from the translation by my old friend and teacher James Moffatt): 'The harvest of the Spirit is love, joy, peace, good temper, kindliness, generosity, fidelity, gentleness, self-control' (Gal. 5.22). He says: 'Love is very patient, very kind. Love knows no jealousy; love makes no parade, gives itself no airs, is never rude, never selfish, never irritated, never resentful; love is never glad when others go wrong, love is gladdened by goodness, always slow to expose, always eager to believe the best, always hopeful, always patient' (I Cor. 13.4-7). He says: 'Bless those who make a practice of persecuting you; bless them instead of cursing them. Rejoice with those who rejoice, and weep with those who weep. Keep in harmony with one another; instead of being ambitious associate with humble folk; never be self-conceited. Never pay back evil for evil to anyone; aim to be above reproach in the eyes

[1] Adam Fox, *Dean Inge* (John Murray, 1960), p. 243.

of all; be at peace with all men, if possible, so far as that depends on you. Never revenge yourselves, beloved' (Rom. 12.14-19). Paul had been brought up in the Pharisaic tradition of piety and propriety. He now depicts a new kind of life, hitherto unknown to the world or only partially seen and dimly grasped. When he declares that such is the Spirit of Jesus, our feet are upon firm historic ground.

6

BEHIND THE GOSPELS

THE composers of our four Gospels were not a committee which, without actually meeting, managed to construct an imaginary figure, Jesus Christ. However uncertain we are, and must be, about details, there is no question that the Gospels rest upon the memories of those who actually knew him. To a limited extent it is plainly possible for us to reach beyond the traditions as we have them to the memories which lie behind them. We owe this distinction between the traditions and the memories to the immense labours of two generations of scholars, but the recognition of it is really a matter of common sense. In this chapter there is nothing that I seek to prove. With all proper hesitation and not relaxing my critical or sceptical propensities I am trying to indicate an outline of an historical situation which we must face honestly. I have written at some length about the uncertainties of historical enquiry but not to offer an excuse for inattention, as if one would say, 'it is all so uncertain and so unlikely that I really cannot bother and puzzle myself with this question of Jesus'. There is no excuse for that intellectual escapism. If we are serious about life, we must seriously consider Jesus.

I plunge into difficulty but, I think, also, into certainty straight away. The story really begins with the work of John the Baptist, whose historicity is undoubted. A gaunt, ascetic figure, he appears by the river Jordan announcing a baptism, which, to quote Dr George Caird, is much as if a king coming to the throne should proclaim an amnesty. The baptism was a symbolic washing away of sins in preparation for some decisive act of God in history and the advent of a mysterious figure known as 'the Coming One'. It required a moral renewal in those baptized. Jesus of Nazareth was baptized by John.

Here, I am afraid, I must be diverted for a moment to consider a question which has puzzled Christians through all the generations. Why should Jesus have come forward for baptism when, as Christians have always asserted, he was 'sinless'? Dogmatists may argue: he was the Son of God, therefore he was sinless. The historian may reply: he was a man, therefore he cannot have been sinless. It is not for the theoretical dogmatist to tell the historian what must have happened. What would 'sinless' mean?

It is quite possible to imagine a child growing into manhood without ever deliberately doing anything which he knew to be wrong. When Jesus quoted the ten commandments to the rich young ruler, the latter replied, 'all these have I kept from my youth up'; in that admirable but rather negative sense sinlessness might be ascribed to him. But if by being sinful we mean entertaining wrong ideas about God and man and acting upon them, it is plain that Jesus received from the Rabbis and the religious environment of his age many ideas from which he later broke. He entered into human life, which then as now is an intricate web of false and true ideas and practices; he was, as the apostle very boldly wrote, 'made sin for us' (II Cor. 5.21). It is proper to be amazed at the sheer intellectual power with which he pierced through all the entanglements of contemporary Judaism to simple and pure religion. The Gospels give no indication of his mental or spiritual development; it was enough to say that 'he grew in favour with God and men' (Luke 2.52), but this was real growth if he was a human being.

78

It may be said, and has been said, that he is not in fact
presented in the Gospels as a perfect character; his alleged
cursing of the fig tree, for instance, his unqualified denun-
ciation of the Pharisees, his threatenings of hell-fire are said
to mar his character. In view of what we know of him
through the Pauline letters these traits do, indeed, seem
'out of character'. It can, I think, be much more than
plausibly shown that here he is misrepresented by the
evangelists. But even so there can be no historical proof
that one of whose life through most of its years we know
nothing at all never did anything which he afterwards re-
gretted. Let it be enough that we can say of him—as we
cannot, in fact, say of any other—that he loved the Lord his
God with all his heart and mind and soul and strength and
his neighbour as himself. He did not wish to be called good,
apparently, for only God is good; he identified himself with
that 'national mission of repentance and hope' of which
John the Baptist was the prophet.

Soon hereafter he comes into Galilee proclaiming that
the hour has struck, that 'the kingdom of God' is at hand.
Here we are in another sort of difficulty, for the phrase 'the
kingdom of God' or 'the kingdom of heaven' is not easily
intelligible to us. It was a Jewish expression and outside
Jewry so awkward that Paul and John, seeking to interpret
the gospel to the Graeco-Roman world, rarely use it and
tend to substitute such phrases as 'the powers of the age to
come' or 'eternal life'. It is one of the proofs of the historical
authenticity of the first three evangelists that they repeat
this phrase again and again; it was an essential part of the
memories on which they draw.

How shall we put the phrase into modern English? It
seems to be used in two contrasting senses, sometimes of
the Consummation of all things beyond history and sometimes of a present experience. An enormous and learned

literature surrounds it, but I think the simplest and nearest English equivalent of the two meanings is often 'heaven' and 'heaven on earth'. Jesus comes into Galilee, then, saying, that the hour has struck and heaven on earth is here.

Heaven on earth is a vague phrase, but it sums up very sufficiently all that modern men, or most modern men, are sure they have not found. Jesus not only declared that heaven on earth was at hand, he claimed to show it at work or in fact. Whether his demonstration all came to nothing in the end is a question we must consider later.

I take for example an incident that has every mark of authenticity. Jesus, we read, had cast out a dumb demon, and the dumb man recovered his speech.[1] As we today ascribe diseases to viruses and germs, the Jews in the time of Jesus ascribed them to demons. We need not doubt that he accepted the ideas current in his time. No diagnosis of his 'miracles' of healing is now possible. We may suppose, if we wish, that in the present case the diagnosis might be hysterical aphasia or dumbness.[2] Perhaps because Jesus used no incantations, nor invoked the name of God, but simply commanded the demon to leave the man, there were some who said that he had power over the demons because he was the representative of the prince of the demons (Beelzebub). That, he says, is nonsense. The devil does not go about undoing the devil's work, but, he continues, 'if I by the finger of God cast out demons, then certainly heaven is invading earth', as a liberating army might cross the frontier.

[1] Luke 11.14 ff.; cf. Matt. 12.22 ff.; Mark 3.22 ff. Those who are interested in the details of literary criticism and a comparison of various forms of what is apparently the same story should consult T. W. Manson, *The Teaching of Jesus* (1931).

[2] See E. R. Micklem, *Miracles and the New Psychology* (1922).

It is plain from the stories that Jesus was embarrassed by the crowds who came to him for healing. He was intensely unwilling to appear before men as a wonder-worker; he absolutely declined to vindicate his calling by some supernatural 'sign'; no sign should be given his generation, he said, except the sign of Jonah the prophet. Jonah had no authority except the spiritual authority of his prophetic word. If men could not recognize the spiritual authority of Moses and the prophets, Jesus is reported to have said at another time, they will not believe though one rise from the dead. In his so-called 'miracles' of healing Jesus saw the dawning of the new age of God and the overthrow of all the powers of evil.

Only to one other act of healing will I refer, for this is most revealing of his character and outlook. The illness called leprosy in the Bible is not, or is not usually, the terrible disease we call by that name today. No diagnosis of biblical cases is now possible. It is certain, however, that a man known as a leper was an outcast from society and from his family; he was unclean, an object of fear and disgust to any Jew brought up to reverence the law of Moses. We read that in some unnamed place a man who was 'full of leprosy' seeing Jesus fell at his feet, saying, 'Sir, you can make me clean if you will', and Jesus, disregarding both the law of Moses and all the instincts of horror in which he had been brought up, put out his hand and touched the man, saying, 'I will; be clean', and the leprosy left him there and then (Luke 5.12 f.). We may suppose, if we will, that the 'leprosy' was some 'hysterical' complaint; we are not required to assume any remarkable breach in natural law, but that man would never forget the one who when he was a leper did not shrink from touching him and touching him healed him. All the gospel is implicit in that story.

In 'the Galilean idyll', as it has been called, Jesus went about healing the sick and the mentally unstable, declaring that the age of God was dawning, that the powers of heaven were invading earth, and calling his hearers to enter this new world of wonder and of grace. Let them set their hearts upon God's rule and not worry about food or clothes, for their heavenly Father who feeds the ravens and without whose cognizance not a sparrow falls to the ground can be trusted to take care of them. He took the most exquisite delight in the flowers of the country-side. Look at the scarlet anemones, he said; they do not toil or spin or worry, but even the great Solomon in all his splendour was not apparelled like one of these. He bore, as he knew, the burden of an overwhelming task, but, though often tired, he was never busy like our great men who, if the secretarial barrier can be broken, may be seen by appointment in due course. His followers were sadly put about when a group of mothers wanted to bring their children to him to be blest; he really was too busy and important for that kind of thing. But he thought otherwise. 'Let the children come to me,' he said; 'don't get in their way; the kingdom of God belongs to them.' On another occasion, he took a little child, set him before them and told them that they must become like little children, for children are completely carefree and know that they are loved.

It would seem that two phrases were almost key-words of his teaching. Of the first our traditional translation is 'be not anxious'; in modern English it is, 'do not worry'. It occurs repeatedly in the traditions of his sayings. The second phrase is usually translated 'be of good cheer' or, as we might say, 'cheer up!'. Jesus called men now, in this present wicked world, to live in what the apostle called 'the glorious liberty of the children of God'. Such was 'the Galilean idyll', very much too good to be true, we say, and tragically contradicted by the fate which was soon to over-take the preacher of this illusory but happy news.

There is much more to be said, but let us not decide too quickly that this is just a pretty tale, for there are plenty of people round about us who would declare it true from their own experience. I think, for instance, of my friend Präses Wilm who wrote an account of his experiences in Dachau Concentration Camp. The first part of the pamphlet is entitled 'Hell in Dachau' and the second part 'Heaven in Dachau'. By a strange paradox those who live most happy and carefree like children that wholly trust and know that they are loved are at the same time those who have given themselves to the alleviation of human misery. How can 'heaven on earth' coexist in the same experience with 'hell on earth'? To this paradox, still keeping close to history, we must now turn.

When I get impatient with church conventions, people often say to me, 'but the Church must have institutions and rules and moral standards that must be obeyed', and I agree with them. None the less, the institutions, rules and moral standards (or conventions) of the Church can often hide Christ from the world. The Jewish Church-State in the time of Jesus was governed in every aspect of the national life by the Law of Moses. For dignity and moral purity there is nothing like it in the pagan world. Jesus was brought up in Judaism; he accepted the Law of Moses as the Law of God; he is even reported to have said that not a comma should be altered in the Law till all was fulfilled, and he may actually have said something of the kind; he never repudiated Judaism; he never suggested that he came to found a new religion; he came to recall Judaism to its true, historic, prophetic function to bring the know-ledge of God to all the world; but if he accepted the Law of Moses, he interpreted it in the spirit of the prophets, not in the spirit of the scribes; he proclaimed, not a new religion but a new age dawning, the powers of heaven invading the dark places of the earth, the throne of Satan shaken and now tottering.

While 'the common people heard him gladly', and his healing ministry seemed the outward sign and seal of the dawning of the new age, 'the kingdom of heaven' or heaven on earth, the opposition of the established church grew ever more bitter until at last it was decided that at all costs he must be silenced. The controversy came to a head over his attitude to the observance of Saturday, the Jewish Sabbath. The strict keeping of the Sabbath was enjoined in the Law of Moses; it was the distinctive mark of Judaism wherever Jews were found throughout the world; it was in a sense the badge of the national religion, and the scribes and rabbis or doctors of the church had hedged about the rules of Sabbath observance in the strictest way.

Jesus did not repudiate the observance of the Sabbath; on that day he attended the synagogue 'as his custom was'. But whereas the official church thought that the keeping of the Sabbath rules was a way of pleasing God, he thought of the Sabbath as God's gracious provision for man; the Sabbath was made for man, not *vice versa*. When his followers being hungry (they must, I think, have been very hungry) plucked ears of corn, rubbed them in their hands and ate them, thus breaking the Sabbath rules against work as the church interpreted it, Jesus did not question the rule but pointed out that when David, the king after God's own heart, as they believed, had been hard pressed and hungry, he had actually eaten the sacramental shew-bread and shared it with his companions. When the church leaders were angry that he healed on the Sabbath—even in the synagogue itself—he asked them whether if one of their beasts fell into a pit on the Sabbath, they would not pull it out at once. Of course they would! Then how much better to perform a work of mercy on a human being on the Sabbath day! He accused his accusers of being 'hypocrites' or play-actors; they were in earnest, certainly, but they were 'putting up a show', as we say; whereas he was dealing with moral and spiritual realities. The denunciations of the scribes and Pharisees in our Gospels are comprehensive and unqualified, but there is evidence that some of them at least saw that he was interpreting the true meaning of their religion. 'Is not this the fast that I have chosen', the prophet had said before him, 'to loose the bands of wickedness, to undo the heavy burdens, and to let the oppressed go free, and that you break every yoke? Is it not to deal your bread to the hungry, and that you bring the poor in their trouble to your house? that you clothe the shivering when you see them, and that you do not hide yourself from your fellow human beings?' (Isaiah 58.6 f.). 'Shall you reign because of your splendid palace?' said Jeremiah to king Shallum. 'Did not your father eat and drink and do judgment and justice; then it was well with him. He judged the cause of the poor and needy? Then it was well with him; was not this to know me, says the Lord?' (Jer. 22.15 f.). That is true religion; that was the true religion of Israel, but to revert to it by abandoning the church rules and scrupulosities of the religious leaders of the day would have meant a religious revolution.

Most of all a revolution in the Jewish attitude to foreigners! The Jews kept themselves most scrupulously apart, neither eating nor marrying with foreigners; they and they alone were the favoured people of heaven. Some of their bitterest feeling was reserved for the Samaritans who were so near them, sharing the Law of Moses, though I think they never treated them with quite the ferocity Christian denominations have shown towards one another in the past. When Jesus was asked 'who is my neighbour whom I ought to love?' he told the story of the good Samaritan. The priest and Levite who 'went by on the other side' may be supposed to have been on important business; besides, the fellow might be dead, and they might become contaminated and unclean by contact with a corpse; but the Samaritan, disregarding all dangers of ceremonial impurity, was moved with human compassion for a fellow human being, though the sufferer was probably a Jew with whom one had no dealings.

There is a story of Jesus' visit to his native town of Nazareth which comes to us in two quite different forms (Luke 4.16-30; Mark 6.1-6). Luke tells us that going into the synagogue on the Sabbath he was called upon to read and expound some passage of Scripture. He took the scroll of Isaiah and read the passage, 'The Lord's Spirit is upon me because he anointed me to declare good news to the poor, he has sent me to announce deliverance to prisoners and sight to the blind, to liberate the victims of oppression, to preach the acceptable year of the Lord.' He then rolled up the scroll, handed it back to the church officer and took his seat. Everyone was looking at him in expectation of what he would say. 'And he began to say to them, this scripture is fulfilled in your hearing today.' Both accounts agree that people took offence. 'Who is he to make such claims? This is only Joseph's son; we know all about him and his family.' Jesus quoted the saying that no prophet is acceptable in his own country and, according to Luke, went on to remind them that during the great drought in Elijah's time, though there were many widows in Israel, it was only to a foreign widow of Sidon that the prophet had been sent, and there were many lepers in Israel in Elijah's time, but the only one he healed was the Syrian, Naaman, a general in the army of the foreigner. In practice the ministry of

Jesus was confined almost exclusively to the Jewish people, but the God he proclaimed, the religion which he lived, knew no barriers of race or colour. The official church was right in judging that his teaching was incompatible with the established Judaism of the day. Jesus might truly claim that he was expounding and fulfilling the religion of the Hebrew prophets, but he was a revolutionary not to be endured. There could be no compromise. How did Jesus view this inevitable clash of principle?

To that question I come in the next chapter. The people heard him gladly, we are told, but they were puzzled too, for living in an occupied country and being brought up in religious nationalism their thinking was politically conditioned. I think we may assume that when Jesus spoke of the fatherhood of God and his care for all his children he carried conviction for the moment; his 'miracles' of healing seemed to corroborate his message that the power of heaven was at work on earth and the throne of Satan tottering. But what about the Romans? There could be no 'heaven on earth' under a despotic Roman occupation. If he was the expected Coming One, they would rally round him, but he had said not a word about the sharpening of swords.

John the Baptist, immured by a tyrant in a lonely fortress, sent a deputation. John had proclaimed the imminence of some decisive act of God. It was good to know that this message was still being proclaimed, good, too, that a few sick people were being healed, but the Coming One must do more than that. Did Jesus claim to be the Coming One? Jesus told the messengers to observe what was happening and to report to John what they saw and heard: 'the blind are receiving back their sight, cripples are walking about, lepers are being cleansed, the deaf are recovering their hearing, the dead are being raised, to the poor the news is being preached—and happy is the man who is not offended [literally 'scandalized'] in me.' That was his answer, not a word about politics, no direct reply to the question put. But the question somehow must be answered; he must say Yes or No to the national hope and expectation. Happy the man who was not offended in him, who could see the hand of God in what was happening and would not confound the kingdom of God with vengeance on the Romans!

In this chapter I am confident that in substance I have kept close to sober and authentic history. There was such a person of Jesus of Nazareth; he taught that God is our Father absolutely to be trusted, so that putting our hearts upon the coming of his kingdom we have no need to worry about anything; there is no doubt that he effected many cures which his contemporaries deemed miraculous; there is no doubt that his sense of religious realities and priorities of his people's mission to the world, made a clash with the official church of the day inevitable, nor could political and even military issues be ultimately avoided. There must have been many who 'hoped it had been he who should redeem Israel', but it all seemed to end in unmitigated disaster and bitter disillusionment.

7

THE ENIGMATIC FIGURE

IN this chapter I must be more hesitant. Jesus had proclaimed the advent of the kingdom or heaven on earth; his
cures had seemed to verify his message; he had quarrelled
with the official church. The outcome cannot be intelligibly
discussed without some consideration of what was in his
mind. Here we are at a stand. It is always a hazardous
undertaking to interpret the mind of any historical figure,
and it would be intolerable presumption to suppose that we
can fathom the mind of Jesus. There is this further difficulty
that here our sources of information or inference are
peculiarly suspect. There is good reason to suppose that predictions of the future put into the lips of Jesus by the
evangelists have sometimes been coloured by the events
that actually occurred, more particularly in the Jewish
rebellion and the destruction of Jerusalem in AD 70. Again,
the evangelists saw the past always in the light of 'the
Resurrection'; to them Jesus was the risen Lord, seated at
the right hand of God, the promised Messiah, the Son of
God; indeed, all the later church dogmas of 'the divinity of
Christ' can be found in embryo within the pages of the New
Testament. When the books of the New Testament were
written he was seen in more than human proportions, and
our necessary attempt to distinguish between the historic
person and the vivid faith of those who wrote about him
and were accustomed to meet 'in his name' is inevitably
hazardous.

There are, however, some statements and traditions which it would be quite unreasonable for even the most critical or sceptical of us to question. I shall try to keep to that which may, I think, be regarded as reasonably certain.

The Temple in Jerusalem built by Herod was widely regarded as one of the wonders of the world. We read that on one occasion Jesus' followers looking at it across the valley exclaimed at its magnificence, and Jesus solemnly assured them that before long not one stone should be left upon another; the whole thing would be utterly destroyed (Mark 13.1 ff.). On another occasion (we are not told the context) he said to the people: 'When you see the clouds gathering in the west, you say, it is going to rain, and it does rain; and when the wind blows from the south, you say it is going to be hot, and so it is; how comes it that you can read the weather but cannot read the clear signs of the times?' (Luke 12.54-56). Perhaps on the same occasion, referring to an event which will have been as little known to the readers of the Gospels in the Graeco-Roman world as it is to us, he said: 'Do you think that those on whom the tower of Siloam fell were outstanding sinners? I tell you that unless you repent you will all die like that' (Luke 13.4 f.).

Jesus, it would seem, saw himself in the line of the Hebrew prophets (Luke 13.33). These predictions of doom upon the people 'unless you repent' are in the strict prophetic tradition. Jesus could see, as we looking back may claim to see, that the Jewish nationalism of the day with its hatred of the Roman oppressor, its scorn of those 'outside the Law', that is, all the outside world, its expectation that God would directly interfere in the course of human history and set the Jews in control of the world, was bound to lead to a clash with the Roman Empire before long, and that in the conflict the Jews would be utterly defeated and their national life destroyed, as indeed happened a few years later. All this must occur 'unless you repent'. Repentance in this connection included a new national attitude towards the Roman Government. The Jews must 'render unto the emperor the things of the emperor', they must 'love their enemies', they must abandon their exclusive nationalism and realize that their wonderful religious tradition as interpreted by the prophets was their message to be taken to all the world. The acceptance of this new attitude was the only way to avert political disaster and national extinction.

We have, then, three elements in the situation to hold together in our minds, first the proclamation that God was acting decisively, the powers of heaven were invading earth, the sick were being healed and men were summoned into 'heaven on earth', a life of utter trust and confidence in the heavenly Father's care of them; second, an unbreachable gulf between religion so understood and the narrow and legalistic religion of the official leaders of the church; third, a prediction that apart from 'repentance' destruction would fall upon the national life with none to escape it. It is, of course, possible that in the early days of his ministry in Galilee, when 'the common people heard him gladly' and before the official church leaders had realized the incompatibility of his way with theirs, Jesus had hoped that the nation would respond to his message, accept his good news, change their minds and hearts towards the Romans and undertake the national calling to bring their knowledge of God to all the world, and only later did he see that disaster could not or would not be avoided. This is surmise, however.

What was his own place and function amid the gathering storms? What were his own 'claims' upon his people? Here we must walk most warily. I will keep to what, amid many questions that cannot be answered with certainty, we may regard as reasonably sure.

There is an enigmatic saying which is not in the least likely to have been invented later: 'I came to cast fire upon the earth. O that it were kindled now! I have a baptism to undergo, and in what distress I am till it is over! Do you think I have come to give peace on earth? On the contrary, division rather!' (Luke 12.49-51). There seems plain contradiction here. What was the proclamation of 'heaven on earth' but the offer of peace to the troubled hearts of men? But here he speaks not of peace but of division and of the fire of judgment. We can see, as we look back with our wisdom after the event, that the Jews at that time were heading for disaster, and that their acceptance or rejection of his message was a decision between life and death. But what was this 'baptism' which he must undergo?

It is told of the apostle Paul in Athens that when the Jews of the synagogue rejected his message he tore his clothes saying to them, 'Then your blood is on your own heads; I am not responsible; from now on I shall make my appeal to the pagans' (Acts 18.6). It is precisely this line which Jesus did not take. It would seem that up to the end he could have escaped the fate that overtook him. He could have given up and gone into retirement; he could have decided that, the forces of officialdom being too much for him in Palestine, he would take his message to the much more liberal-minded Jews dispersed round the Mediterranean and especially in Alexandria. It is reported that at the very end of his life some Greek-speaking Jews wanted to see him; he replied by sending them a parable: 'Unless a grain of wheat dies when it falls into the ground, it stays just what it is; but if it dies, it brings forth a crop' (John 12.24). Jesus went up on his last journey to Jerusalem under no illusions; he told his group of followers that if they came with him, they took their lives in their hands. The sequel is not really intelligible if in fact he had described to his followers in detail beforehand what would happen to him in Jerusalem, but deeply embedded in the tradition (far too deeply to be a later invention) is his conviction that he 'must' die. The earliest Church, probably but not quite certainly following the teaching of Jesus himself, interpreted this necessity in terms of the prophecy in Isaiah 53 of the Suffering Servant of the Lord, who was to bear the sins of many, to make his grave with the wicked and afterwards see the satisfaction of his soul in the redemption accomplished by his death.

It is an equally certain element in the tradition that Jesus spoke of coming back after his death. In the Gospels we find ascribed to him very definite predictions both of resurrection and of a coming again on the clouds of heaven. These two ideas are different and are not found combined. We may take it as probable that these definite predictions are later interpretations of his much vaguer references to a coming back, the one in terms of what actually happened, the other in terms of current apocalyptic hopes. We can only be certain, I think, that he spoke of his death as in some way necessary to the purposes of God, and that he spoke also of some coming back again.

It is quite certain that he did not go about proclaiming himself to be the 'Messiah' of Jewish national expectation. Had he done so, the people would have understood this at least partly in a political sense, the police or military would quickly have been called in, and the Jewish authorities at the end would have had no difficulty in finding a sufficient charge to bring against him before the Roman governor.

A phrase, however, that was constantly on his lips was 'Son of Man'. It recurs constantly in the Gospels and in general is a clear mark of authentic historical reminiscence, for, translated into Greek or Latin (or English), the words hardly make sense, and the phrase was virtually dropped when the Christian faith was presented to the pagan world. A whole literature gathers round its interpretation. We can assert with much confidence that it bears some relation or reference to the passage in Daniel where the seer in a vision beholds the great empires of the past and of his own day under the form of beasts, and then sees one 'like a son of man' who represents the persecuted saints of Judaism and who receives from God the empire of the world. Did Jesus think of himself as Daniel's Son of Man become historical, as Son of God or as Messiah? If so, how did he interpret these great titles?

It may be a matter of much significance that none of these names is necessarily the title of a single individual. The Son of Man in Daniel represents the saints or faithful remnant in the days of persecution; Israel is spoken of in the Old Testament as God's Son; 'Messiah' (or *'Christos'* in Greek) merely means 'anointed', and all members of the Christian Church were supposed to be anointed (I John 2.20). If publicly or in his own thought Jesus applied these titles to himself, he was not necessarily separating himself from any who would stand with him. I venture with proper hesitation, yet with some confidence, to hazard the suggestion that if we ask the question, 'What did Jesus think about himself?', almost the right answer is, 'He did not think about himself at all.' He was throughout concerned, if I may so put it, with the Father's will, with the task he had to do, the calling he must fulfil, but not at all with metaphysical questions about his own person. John the Baptist had announced the imminence of God's decisive act of history; Jesus declared that the kingdom of heaven or the powers of the age to come were *already* invading this present age. This was indicated by his driving out the

94

powers of darkness in the healing of the sick and the deranged. He knew—it is impossible to write here without presumption, but we must try to understand as best we may—he knew that in sending the kingdom God had sent him to declare it and manifest it in word and deed; so far as we can see, he lived in unclouded sonship with the Father; but, after all, he called others into that sonship, which is heaven on earth, and he sent his followers out to declare the arrival of the kingdom and like himself to heal the sick. He spoke with immense and astonishing authority; where prophets had said, 'Thus saith the Lord', he said, 'Moses said . . . but I say unto you'; but he spoke because he knew, because he saw, not because he was thinking of the dignity and authority of his personal office. He went up to Jerusalem deliberately to die for his people, but he called his followers to come with him and be ready to die with him. We may inevitably call him the unique or, to use the biblical phrase, the only-begotten Son of God, and surrounded by his devoted but constantly misunderstanding followers he must have seen as plainly as we can that only through him could they enter the kingdom or know heaven on earth; but whereas much scholarship has been devoted to 'the self-consciousness of Jesus', he was perhaps the most unselfconscious man who ever lived; his meat and drink, as he is alleged to have said, was to do the will of the Father. If we would understand him, we should ask not what he thought about himself, what claims he made for himself, but what he conceived to be the will of God for him.

His disciples would not have been so utterly shattered by the disaster of the Crucifixion if, as the Gospels would have us believe, he had really predicted in detail exactly what would happen. It seems quite certain however that he came to see, if he did not see from the beginning, that the decisive act of God involved his death; hence deliberately and with no illusions he went up to Jerusalem to challenge his enemies in the seat of their power, fully anticipating death and assuring his followers, perhaps in cryptic terms, that in some way he would come back.

We have to contemplate an enormous paradox. I have written of 'the Galilean idyll', the glad and carefree message that the powers of evil were being already overthrown, that this world, so long an 'occupied country', was being invaded by a liberating army. The 'miracles' of healing were a proof of this; heaven on earth was proclaimed; God was utterly trustworthy; let men put aside all worry, take no thought for food and clothing, for God was to be trusted to look after all his children. That was the message. Jesus never went back on it, and, what is equally astonishing, in spite of all that happened to him, that teaching was preserved by the Church as true and the word of life. Yet Jesus himself who had brought the good news, and who, if anyone, might trust God to see that he came to no harm, was to die under conditions of extreme horror, and in spite of all the Galilean teaching anyone who stood with him must be willing to share his fate. We utterly miss the point of the paradox if on the one hand we pick beautiful and comforting texts out of the Sermon on the Mount and, on the other, explain the death of Jesus as due to some mysterious transaction between the pre-existent Son of God and his eternal Father. It is history, not sentiment or speculation, which sets the problem for us. Why *must* Jesus die? Was not his fate the final denial of all that he had taught in Galilee?

There is a story that when Jesus spoke of his coming sufferings, his friend Peter rebuked him. 'Do not speak like that,' he said. I think that Jesus' almost fierce reply, 'Get behind me, Satan,' indicates how much he felt the force of Peter's protest. Should not we, who are people of common sense, have said much what Peter said? We should very sensibly have presumed to point out that, after all, his work was only just begun, that the movement he was to inaugurate had hardly started, that even those closest to him were very far from understanding him, that at the very least he must write a book and set up an organization with proper committees and a clear constitution before he could personally be spared. His going up to Jerusalem was, of course, an act of enormous courage, but it was also an act of faith which to our normal judgment would seem mad. It is conceivable that part of the agony in the Garden of Gethsemane was the doubt whether this 'cup' could really be the Father's will for him.

It is extremely probable that he had meditated long on the passage in Isaiah 53 where it is said of the Servant of the Lord (whether to be conceived as an individual or a faithful remnant is not clear) that he should bear the sins of the many, go down to a shameful death, and afterwards see of the travail of his soul and be satisfied. It was written of him later that 'for the joy that was set before him he endured the Cross' (Heb. 12.2), but we must regard his death as a staggering act of faith. With his work hardly begun, as it seemed, with his disciples still so far from understanding him that they were concerned about matters of precedence in the kingdom of God, with no one to stand by him in the end, with deliberation and in serenity he went to a terrible and protracted death in the confidence that through his obedience to the felt will of God the decisive act of God in human history must be accomplished. Was this the faith of a fanatic, or was he right? That is a question men have answered differently.

We may well here consider 'the Last Supper', as we call it. Two preliminary observations will be in place. First, I think there may still be a custom amongst schoolboys and villains that when a most solemn engagement is to be entered into, each will drink a drop of the other's blood, but for the civilized world in general the idea that a solemn covenant should be 'sealed in blood' has long since disappeared. Among the Jews in the time of Jesus, however, the idea was living and connected with the covenants between God and man of which we read in the Old Testament. Second, civilized men when they have entered into a close bond with one another, especially if they have previously been estranged, will very naturally take one another by the hand. The handshake may properly be called a sacramental act, because it is a physical or material action which expresses, conveys and seals a spiritual agreement. 'We have not only agreed, but we have shaken hands on it.'

Of Jesus' Last Supper with his friends we have five differing accounts in the New Testament, or six if we include the Fourth Gospel, which makes no direct reference here to bread or wine. We should not, at least we almost certainly should not, think of Jesus as deliberately instituting some new rite. He was using the ritual of bread and wine familiar in Jewish households and doubtless familiar in his past companionship with his disciples. What made this particular meal for ever memorable was, of course, partly that it was the last meal he took with his friends on earth, but even more the words he spoke. Amid many uncertainties it may be taken as certain that he broke the round loaf and gave it to his companions with the words 'This is my body'; and it is probable but not certain (for this does not appear in the shorter and probably authentic text of Luke) that in passing round the cup of wine he made reference to a new covenant between God and man in his blood. If we would interpret what he meant, we must start on the assumption that whatever he said must have been intelligible to those who were actually present on that occasion.

I write here with a little confidence. When he gave them the loaf saying, 'This is my body'. they must, I think, have understood him to be saying in effect, 'I am giving myself to you and for you', and to them the bread, like the handshake, will have been sacramental; they will have understood that he was expressing, conveying and sealing his self-giving for them and 'for many'. If he spoke of the cup as a covenant-cup in his blood, they must have understood him to mean that in his death there was being inaugurated a new relationship between God and man, and that in receiving it they were taken up into this new covenant.

The sequel, the story of the passion, is well known to us, though in detail there are uncertainties. He remains a majestic figure through all the horror of the mocking, the torture and the crucifixion. The way of Jesus being rejected by the Jewish nation, the Jewish war and the destruction of the national life became politically inevitable. It is said (surely an historical reminiscence) that when he was being led to death he was met by women in tears (women, by the way, seem to have shown much more courage than the men when the crisis came). To these tearful women he said, 'Women of Jerusalem, weep not for me; weep for yourselves' (Luke 23.28). Christian piety, which expresses pity for Jesus (if I may be allowed another aside), is far astray; he never asked for pity; he prayed only that God's will might be done; 'The cup that the Father hath given me, shall I not drink it?' (John 18.11).

When he saw what he had done, Judas Iscariot (to his credit, shall we say?) committed suicide. Peter, who had publicly denied any acquaintance with his master and his friend, must have felt much as Judas did. Consider what we must suppose to have been in the mind of Jesus' nearest followers: they had loved him; they had loved his teaching; he was their master and their dear friend; when the crisis came, they had all run away and left him, and he had died a horrible and shameful death alone. Not only had they lost their friend, but everything he had taught in Galilee must now seem nonsense. Those 'miraculous' healings had been but a flash in the pan; all that teaching about God's care of his children and his utter reliability, when put to the test, had been proved false. They had lost their friend, and they had lost their God. It must, I think, have been like that with them on Good Friday afternoon.

We now come to the most serious, the most searching and the most unavoidable question which any modern man with a sense for religion must ask himself. Was Jesus' teaching about God true, or just an idyllic phantasy? Was Jesus right in his proclamation that God was acting decisively in history, or did he suffer the delusion of a fanatic? Did God in fact vindicate Jesus, or is he dead and done for?

8

THE VINDICATION

WE have the evidence of a reliable contemporary that shortly after the death of Jesus a very large number of persons, some of whom are named, and most of whom were alive when the record was made, either saw or thought they saw him alive again (I Cor. 15.3 ff.). Paul ends his account by saying, 'finally I saw him myself'. This proves nothing, but is a sufficiently attested historical fact and must be accepted as such.

For a long time I was disposed to think that the biblical narratives of the empty tomb might very possibly be the, perhaps unconscious, inventions of piety and cult. I have been persuaded by Professor C. H. Dodd[1] that the story of the empty tomb belongs to the earliest strata of tradition. We must take it for an historical fact that, however it be explained, his body disappeared. The strongest evidence for this is negative: the early Christian witness was wholly based on the alleged fact that Jesus was risen from the dead. If his enemies could have produced his dead body, the Christian movement would have collapsed at once.

But this, again, of itself proves nothing. What happened to his body is a question for speculation or devout theory; it is not open to investigation. We must accept the fact that the tomb was found empty or at least that his body disappeared, but that of itself leads to no conclusion. It is

[1] C. H. Dodd, *Historical Tradition in the Fourth Gospel*, pp. 140 ff.

certain, however, that the Christians from the earliest times celebrated Sunday as 'the Lord's Day'. He was crucified on Friday; he rose, they said, on Sunday. This conception introduces serious difficulties for us. The traditional view is that he remained dead from the Friday till the Sunday morning; he 'descended into hell', that is, into Sheol, the underworld of the departed. We cannot easily bring that idea within the framework of our scientific thought. There was, however, a group of very early Christians (the Quarto-decimans they were called) who celebrated his death and also his resurrection on the Friday. There is a trace of this belief in the New Testament itself, for there is a legend that on the night of his death the departed saints were seen walking in the streets of Jerusalem (Matt. 27.52 f.). Now if the departed saints were risen, it could only be because Jesus himself was risen and had thrown open the forbidding gates of Sheol. We are here in the realm of what is to us mythology. I think the facts are met, but not explained, if we assume that he died on the Friday and passed thereby into the world invisible, but that his tomb was found to be empty or his body was found to have disappeared, and he was first seen, or believed to have been seen, alive on the Sunday morning.

It is not, I think, possible without intellectual legerdemain or special and unconvincing pleading to harmonize all the Resurrection stories. It is, however, as certain as can be that within a very short time of his death many people saw him or believed that they had seen him, and that within a month or so, except in the case of the apostle Paul, these appearances came to an end. The astonishing confidence of the early Christian witness is evidence that the faithful were convinced beyond a peradventure that their crucified Master was alive? Should their testimony have any weight with us in this scientific age?

102

Their good faith is not in question. We are not, however, required to believe that if *per impossibile* the Press had been present with its cameras and flashlights it would have been able to photograph the vision. I am prepared to believe that the cameras would have proved wholly un-revealing. These appearances were no doubt decisive for those who saw them; for us they cannot be decisive. By this I do not at all mean that we should reject these narratives as mere fables, but our religious faith cannot rest upon what other people are reported to have seen. It is narrated that Jesus himself once said, 'If they will not believe Moses and the prophets, neither will they believe though one rise from the dead' (Luke 16.31). Religious faith is a matter of insight, not of second-hand report.

On those terms let me revert to the dilemma I posed earlier. How are we to relate the message of John the Baptist which Jesus repeated, the 'Galilean idyll', the proclamation that the kingdom of heaven or heaven on earth was at hand, that God was about to act decisively in the course of human history, that the old world, the realm of 'Satan', was tottering and that the age of God, of heaven on earth, was about to supersede it—how are we to relate this picture to the fact that Jesus himself died under con-ditions of horror and shame, deserted by his friends and, as it must have seemed, deserted by God himself? How are we to explain the fact that for millions from every continent and in every age down to our own the Cross has become the symbol of hope, of victory, of undying love?

Most men do not consider this question at all and, of those who do, there are some who set it all aside as the self-deception of unbalanced minds. But this is intellectual cowardice. Those who do not take Christianity seriously are either themselves not serious or must themselves be willing sufferers from self-deception. It is always possible

103

to 'explain away' the Resurrection stories; it is not possible to explain away that shaking of the earth which has followed the death of Jesus.

By taking Christianity seriously I do not mean undertaking a survey of Christian doctrines; I mean, rather, that in our thought about life and death and the mystery that surrounds our human existence we should give due weight to Jesus as a figure in history and to those events which followed his death and can be directly and properly ascribed to him. There are those who have thought that Jesus, in his expectation of some decisive intervention of God in human affairs, was mistaken and disappointed. If he expected something like 'the end of the world' or even an event as spectacular as the exploding of an atom bomb, he was certainly mistaken. It is, however, extremely doubtful whether such was his expectation. We can only assert with confidence that he believed that in the mysterious purposes of God his own death was involved, and that after his death he would in some way come again or come back. This return was interpreted by some in terms of a Resurrection and by others in terms of a Second Coming; the two ideas have been combined in later Christian thought, but they are not combined in the New Testament.[1] We should, I think, be wise to suppose that he was certain of God's will for him and was well content without speculation to leave the further issue in the Father's hands.

But what in fact did happen? We are not to minimize the importance of the Resurrection appearances, for without them the rise of the Christian Church is not to be explained. I am willing to believe that they were 'subjective' in the sense that no camera would have recorded them, but (this is the decisive question!) did the disciples see

[1] C. H. Dodd, *The Historical Tradition in the Fourth Gospel*, p. 414.

him, or think they saw him, although in fact he was not
present with them, or were they so vividly conscious that he
was with them that they actually saw, or seemed to see, him
bodily in their midst?

That question we cannot answer without considering the
sequel. That brings us to the troublesome and ambiguous
question of 'church history'. A great many people who are
much drawn to the person of Jesus are contemptuous of the
Christian Church for reasons that are not wholly to their
discredit. The Old Testament is often treated as the record
of the Hebrews' gradual growth in the understanding of
God. If we took the prophetic view of the narratives, however, we might better describe the Old Testament as the
record of the Hebrews' constant disloyalty to their God.
Church history is often regarded as the gradual working out
of the implications of the life and work of Jesus for human
thought and human history. If we took a prophetic view
we might better describe it as the record of man's constant
failure to understand what Jesus meant and what he stood
for. Church history is from this aspect the most heart-
breaking of studies which men can undertake. When, therefore, I speak of the sequel to the Resurrection appearances,
I mean only those events in church history and altogether
outside church history which are plainly and directly due
to Jesus, what he was and what he did.

We have considered the plight of the disciples on the
evening of Good Friday, their leaderlessness, their most
imperfect understanding of what Jesus had taught, the
shattering of their faith that a new age was dawning. In the
light of this the rapid spread of the Christian religion over
the known world in spite of the imperfection and inade-
quacy of its members and the attempt of the Government
from time to time to suppress it altogether, and then the
acceptance of this religion as the official faith of the still

unshaken Roman Empire in about three hundred years—
that is something as nearly incredible as it is historically
certain. The Resurrection appearances of Jesus, however
decisive for the few who saw him, cannot possibly account
for the astonishing sequel in European history. We should
not sentimentally idealize the early Christians, but there is
no doubt that there sprang up all round the Mediterranean
world and even further afield little groups or fellowships
which offered the world a new kind of life, and which were
united by a conviction that God is our Father wholly to be
trusted, that Jesus the Christ was really present with them
in their corporate experience, and that the mutual care of
one another and the showing of brotherhood to all mankind
was their appointed duty. For the most part they were
'nobodies', as we say, without political influence, without
financial power, without prestige of any sort. It is an extra-
ordinary story, but it is not to be questioned.

It is true that once Christianity became the accepted and
official imperial faith a great change came, the 'first fine
careless rapture' faded, the bishops developed into state
officials, it became the easy and proper thing to call oneself
a Christian. From that time to this the Church when armed
with political power has been guilty of atrocities. Many
non-Christians have been morally far more respectable
than many Christians. Even so and while it is a great
mistake to romanticize the Middle Ages, there have always
been 'the saints', such as the missionaries who brought the
gospel to Britain, whether from Ireland or from Italy;
there have always been communities (in those days usually
monastic communities) which seemed to their members to
be colonies of heaven on earth, such as the Iona community
led by St Columba. The christianizing of the savage tribes
of Europe, however partial and incomplete, is a remarkable
chapter in European history, and there has rarely been such

a flowering of religious and technical philosophy as round about the thirteenth century. The most sceptical are willing to admit that the Christian religion did much for the life and morals of Europe, but they are apt to avoid the difficult question how all this change in Europe arose through the work of a few not very educated and wholly disillusioned Jews whose teacher and master had suffered a felon's death at Roman hands.

It is now customary to say that we are living in a post-Christian age. This makes sense if we compare modern with mediaeval European civilization, but the sense is very limited. Except in a few relatively backward countries of Europe and America, political power with social prestige has been taken from the Church. But political power and social prestige have nothing to do with the religion of Jesus. At the present moment all over the world, and perhaps more obviously and purely in Asia and in Africa than in Europe and America (as most certainly in Russia), there are little groups and fraternities really comparable in their common faith, their mutual service and their outlook upon the world with those groups which constituted the early Church in the Mediterranean world. We are not in a position to ascribe all this to superstition, to fanaticism, to what Germans calls *Schwärmerei* or irrational enthusiasm. I am not seeking to prove the truth of Christianity from its successes; indeed, I am not sure that I know what is meant by 'the truth of Christianity', but I am concerned to show that when we speak of 'the Resurrection' of Jesus, we have in mind much more than the stories and legends of his appearances to his disciples after his death.

The world in these days is everywhere in turmoil; militant atheism reigns over a large part of the earth's surface; Asia and Africa suffer the convulsions of new life and vision. It might seem an extreme and stupid paradox to suggest that

107

all this is part of the story of 'the Resurrection', but I think it is not paradox. Communism has sometimes been described as a vast Christian heresy; it might more properly be called a Jewish heresy, for Karl Marx has been called, not wholly inappropriately, 'the last of the Hebrew prophets'. Communism in practice we may abominate as a tyranny and reject in theory as an economic fallacy; but if we look deeper, we see that it has made its appeal as a vision and ideal. Every recorded age of human history hitherto has been a system of privilege, whether of birth or power or wealth. In our more genial and perhaps less effective institution of a Welfare Society we are attempting to redress the wrongs of the underprivileged. Communism is in principle warfare against privilege, whether of race, birth, property or colour. The 'anti-colonialism' that today sweeps Africa and Asia and often takes such tragic, cruel and even ridiculous forms is part of this same world-wide determination to end the day of privilege, a conviction which Christians might express by the principle that all persons and all peoples are of equal worth in the sight of God. It may be centuries rather than decades before a new and stable world-order is established, but we cannot doubt, I think, that this new world-order when it comes will be far more 'Christian' than any kind of peace the world has known before. What is the source of this conviction that privilege must be swept away, that all men and all peoples have an equal right to share in the good things of life? It comes unquestionably from the Bible. I for one should not hesitate to say that the present turmoil and seething of the world, though marred by the folly, the sinfulness, the blindness, the malice of men, is part of the ferment that was brought into the world by Jesus. God is plainly vindicating Jesus.

One other aspect of Christianity the serious thinker must take into account. I shall call it for convenience 'the Salvation **Army**' aspect. It is twofold. The Salvation Army does a great work of social rescue; this may be taken as representative of the provision of schools, hospitals and charity in the days before the State (under the pressure of Christian and humanitarian influences) largely assumed these responsibilities, and of the immense charitable work such as Christian Aid and the work for the refugees still carried on by Christians. The primary task of the Salvation Army, however, is the rescue and conversion of individual persons. A generation ago Harold Begbie in *Broken Earthenware* vividly retold many stories of men brought back from the depths of degradation to self-respect, to the glad and glorious 'liberty of the children of God', as Paul called it. But in fact there are unnumbered men and women in all walks of life in this land and in others who have undergone no such spectacular 'conversion' as those of whom Begbie wrote, and who yet would like to bear witness to what Jesus has meant to their inner selves, but of these things one does not speak readily nor easily find words:

> but something sealed
> The lips of that evangelist.

The mission work of the Salvation Army offers a kind of ocular demonstration of that which is akin to the experiences of very many. When the name of Jesus is still so powerful to heal, we may not think of him as dead and done for.

Such facts may not be disputed, yet all this, it may be said, is due to the influence of Jesus. Alexander the Great, Julius Caesar, William the Conqueror, Napoleon altered the course of history; the influence of Jesus has been both wider and deeper; that is all; there is no proof here, it will be said, that he is 'risen from the dead' and is still alive.

I am not sure that I want to answer this, and certainly

we are not in the sphere of logical demonstration. 'Influence' is a difficult idea. The word by derivation means a kind of in-flowing. When my friend influences me, something from him or some element in him enters into me. He can continue to influence me when he is dead and buried, and it is difficult to imagine an activity without an agent. It might be said, I suppose, that I am influenced by a memory, but, not having had the experience, I do not know what dying is, and therefore I am arguing in the dark. I am not in the least anxious to maintain, nor do I in fact believe, that when we die, that is the end of us, whereas in the one and only case of Jesus he died and that was not the end of him. I am only concerned with spiritual facts which can be quite easily verified by talking to any real Christians. Even if they are articulate, their expressions will vary much, but they would all say that their life is not lived in accordance with a memory of some one who lived nineteen centuries and more ago but by an inspiration and a power which they would ascribe to the living Christ or to the Spirit of Jesus or the presence of God as he is made known through Jesus. It is always possible to urge that they live under a delusion, but I doubt whether that can be sincerely urged. Delusion is the basis of neurosis, and the last people in the world whom I should call neurotic are real Christians. It is not only in world-events but also in the lives of individual men that God has vindicated and is vindicating Jesus. His enemies thought that they had vanquished him; they were mistaken; it is he who is victorious over them. That, I take it, is what 'the Resurrection' means.

Let me come at the matter in a different way. We cannot describe the scent of new-mown hay; we can only exhort our town-dwelling friends to come and smell it. 'I have felt a Presence', wrote Wordsworth of his experience among the hills, the lakes, the vistas of the country that he loved. It was a quite indemonstrable Presence. To how many, however, have his words brought home that which in some dim way they themselves have felt! It would be idle to take an unbeliever saying to him, 'if you will stand with me above Coniston, you will feel a Presence'. What we can say, I think, is this, that if a man be not wholly insensitive to spiritual impressions, and if he have not already made up his mind what one can and what one cannot experience, then if he will stand above Coniston and feel the wind blow upon him, and watch the shadows of the clouds upon the hills, and take note of the flowers at his feet, and will be still and let the prospect speak to him, he will know that Presence, however little he may be able to find words for his experience. We must cultivate our spiritual awareness.

I wish I could say, 'if only you will come to church next Sunday, you will be aware of the presence of the living Jesus', but that is a promise I cannot make for two reasons in particular. The first is that to whatever type of church you might elect to go, you would very likely be 'put off' by habits or rites unfamiliar to you. The second reason is involved in the obscurity of this phrase 'the presence of the living Jesus'. There are many devout Christians who would say that this phrase vividly and exactly describes their deepest and even constant awareness or experience. Other Christians, equally devout, would not use this expression naturally, but with precisely the same meaning, as I suppose, would speak of the felt presence of the Holy Spirit.

Here one is certainly in the field of confession, not of demonstration. Wordsworth, in what is sometimes described as a pantheistic rather than Christian mood, was aware of that 'Presence far more deeply interfused'. He could only tell of his experience in the best words which he could find. I myself can think of many homes, many gatherings of friends, many occasions in church as well as many private occasions like that of Wordsworth alone among the hills, when I have been deeply aware of what is perhaps best called a Presence. A Presence of what? The Presence of God or the Presence of Jesus? I think I should say the Presence or Spirit of God if I wanted to stress its mysterious and august and ineffable quality, and the Presence or Spirit of Jesus if I wanted to define its ethical and personal and gracious character. I feel sure of this too, that if I took my agnostic friends to these homes or these occasions, they also, unless quite insensitive to spiritual impressions, would know what I meant and feel what I have felt, however they might try and fail to find words in which to indicate this experience.

There is the familiar story of the person who being suddenly confronted by a giraffe declared categorically that no such beast existed. There are some who would not believe in ghosts even if they saw one and heard the clanking chains, for they are persuaded that ghosts are figments of the imagination. Many people today are convinced—not from experience but because of their theories of life and of the world—that any sense of the Presence of God is a fiction of this kind. Let us admit that many so-called 're-ligious experiences' should be dismissed as due to neurosis or hysteria. We may not set our critical judgment in abeyance when we come to religion. But as one who has never attended a séance is in no position to dismiss Spiritualism as mere nonsense, and one who has never handled a test-tube is in no condition to deny the findings of the scientists, so one who has never exposed himself sincerely and with an open mind to the experience of Wordsworth or the experience of Christians, and who takes upon himself to rule out 'religious experience' as self-deception is acting insincerely and unscientifically. It *might* be true that Jesus is alive and his presence is felt by men today, and the agnostic *might* find it to be true if with an open mind and a willingness to be persuaded he attended High Mass or went into the slums with the Salvation Army. Much irreligion (but not all) is due to sheer laziness and unwillingness to be persuaded.

I may seem to be wandering—and indeed I have wandered far from the early traditions of the empty tomb; but if I had confined myself to a discussion of the Resurrection narratives, I should hardly have been discussing the Resurrection. We do not know, and cannot know, precisely what happened at the Resurrection, but the historic fact, whatever it was, taken by itself in isolation would merely be a marvel. It is not to be isolated from what preceded and what followed it. Christians view the Cross, the Resurrection and Pentecost or the coming of the new life into the world as one single event, one decisive act of God, in three aspects or stages. There is not the Cross without the Resurrection—that would be the death of hope. There is not the Resurrection without Pentecost—that would be but a Pyrrhic victory, a personal victory for Jesus and the failure of his mission. Whatever precisely may have occurred, what took place convinced the disciples, beyond all doubt or question, that although apparently Jesus on Calvary had died deserted by the God in whom he trusted, now God had said 'Yes' to Jesus, and 'in the Spirit' Jesus was still present with his people. The Resurrection stands not for the resuscitation of a dead body (as in the story of Lazarus), but for the divine vindication of Jesus' teaching, a victory through death over death and over all the powers of darkness, a new age begun for all mankind.

But would it have made any difference to our religious life if Jesus after delivering his message had slipped away, as he could have done—had retired, let us say, to the Jewish colony in Egypt, and died like others in his bed?

113

9

AN INTELLIGIBLE THEOLOGY

WITH some internal disquiet I have headed this chapter 'an intelligible theology'. I wonder how many readers have already dropped by the wayside; some, I hope, will have persevered and not without pantings and groanings and grave hesitations will have come with me so far. In writing about Jesus heretofore I have tried to keep to facts, either facts of history or facts of inward experience in the individual heart. How, it will be asked, are these facts to be related to what we hear in church, to the doctrines and dogmas of Christianity. How are we to think of Jesus?

I said in my preface that my argument, such as it is, is 'existential', by which I meant that it is addressed to the whole person, not to the intellect alone. To discuss theology is an excellent device for avoiding God. To talk about God is a fascinating intellectual experience; to speak to God or to let God speak to us is a shattering experience. 'If there is nothing that can so hide the face of our fellow man from us as morality can,' wrote Martin Buber, 'so religion can hide from us as nothing else can the face of God.'[1] I may put into words the Gospel, but only those who need it will understand what I am writing. The understanding of the Gospel requires great intellectual and personal integrity, but in itself it is quite simple, and to it all the doctrines or theories of the theologians are altogether secondary. Let me put it as best I can.

[1] *Between Man and Man* (Fontana ed., 1961), p. 36.

There is no reasonable doubt that Jesus taught that he was giving his life 'a ransom for many' (Mark 10.45), that his death was to seal a new covenant between God and man, that his death was *necessary* to the accomplishment of his task. This raises many difficulties in our minds, for we cannot easily see either historical or theological necessity in his death. In particular, the modern man is not so much offended as completely baffled by the traditional Christian teaching that men are saved 'by the blood of Jesus', that the Cross was some sort of mysterious transaction which enabled God to forgive the sins of men.

We can see that his death was inevitable if he persisted on his chosen course. Between the narrow, nationalist, legalistic piety of the religious leaders of Israel and the free, prophetic, universal message of Jesus there could be no compromise. He could, indeed, have gone into retirement or gone abroad to appeal to the more liberal Jews of Egypt and the Dispersion. When he deliberately 'set his face to go to Jerusalem' on that last journey to challenge his opponents in the seat of their power, we may say that his doom was sealed. He entered the Temple, we are told, and drove out the money-changers and their cattle, quoting the declaration of the prophet that the Temple was to be a house of prayer for all nations; it had been turned into a bazaar. For some days he taught in the Temple with such popular support that the authorities were afraid to arrest him, but they must stop him at all costs. If they could trump up some passable charge that he was claiming to be Messiah, the king, they could get the Roman Government to do their work for them, and there was always lynch-law, as the case of Stephen later showed. The historical inevitability of his death we can understand; it is its alleged theological importance that we find so puzzling.

In this matter we may not claim to fathom the mind of

115

Jesus. Though it may seem to us that his work was only begun, and that his further presence and teaching were of vital importance if his message was to win acceptance and be understood, he was plainly persuaded that it was his Father's will that he should die, that his death was essential to that breaking through of God which would usher in the new age, the kingdom of God or heaven on earth. If none would stand by him, he must go his way alone, misunderstood and derelict. It is likely that he thought of himself and his calling in connection with the righteous Sufferer who is the subject of so many psalms and the Servant of the Lord of whom Isaiah speaks. Does this make sense to us?

Let us come at the matter from an altogether different angle. Jesus had said in Galilee that God is the heavenly Father whose love for his children knows no bounds, that God is utterly to be trusted, and that none can escape his care and interest. This he might have continued with general acceptance to say elsewhere. Had this been all, he would have been *par excellence* the philosopher of the love of God; some record of his teaching might have come down to us, and we, more particularly in these days, should have regarded it wistfully and even affectionately as a remote romance; the hard facts of the world are not compatible with this delightful day-dreaming. But suppose for a moment that God really is as Jesus said he was, how could that truth possibly be brought home to man?

Jesus not merely taught the love of God for all his creatures; that love was also incarnated in his own attitude to men. We can usually distinguish clearly between a prophet and what he taught; but with Jesus the person and the teaching were identified; in what he was and said and did, he was himself the grace of God manifested in a human personality. We must connect God with goodness;

there is, as we might put it, a Friend behind phenomena; but how much does God care? A benign Providence is a comfortable philosophy, but how could I be persuaded, how could I dare think, that God loves me? I will cite once again the words spoken or written (I forget which) by T. R. Maltby that Jesus on the Cross 'with arms outstretched embraced the soul of every man for better for worse, for richer for poorer, and death never shall us part'. Having loved his own, he loved them unto the end, and what an appalling end it was in shame and desertion and torture and brutality and horror! If a love of men to the uttermost is to be believed, it must be shown in flesh and blood and upon the stage of history. Jesus has made credible the love of God by showing it. It is not really credible, I think, that the Power and Wisdom of God should be so great, and that his good will should be less than that which a human being showed!

Three famous parables form the fifteenth chapter of Luke's Gospel, the lost sheep, the lost coin and 'the prodigal son', as we call it. God in the teaching of Jesus is not like a shepherd who sitting comfortably at home should regret extremely that one of his sheep is lost. The good shepherd will go in search of the lost sheep 'till he find'. The initiative is with the shepherd; the initiative in man's salvation is with God; it is that divine initiative which is at once mirrored and made credible in Jesus' journey to Jerusalem to die.

Those three parables, the lost sheep, the lost coin, the lost son indicate not merely the divine initiative but the peculiar and particular love of the Father for the lost. When in Luther's vivid imagination the devil would come and taunt him, 'Thou art a sinner and therefore thou art damned', Luther would triumphantly refute the devil out of his own mouth, for to be a sinner and to know that one is

117

a sinner is to know oneself within the care and love of God, since Christ has died for sinners. The Cross of Jesus was the manifestation in time of the love that is eternal. That is the Gospel.

The old traditional doctrines of the Atonement represent Jesus either as the Victor over the devil or as the sacrificial 'Lamb of God'. We cannot think in those terms now. Besides, the two ideas, belonging to totally different worlds of thought, are logically incompatible with one another. But, as Professor John Knox has pointed out, they correspond with man's two deepest spiritual needs, the need for deliverance and the need for forgiveness.[1] I feel assured that we all, unless we be blinded by pride or self-deception, realize our need for deliverance and for forgiveness. It is the sick, not the healthy, who need a physician. Jesus may be of romantic interest only to those who are unaware of any deep spiritual need. Those who have found deliverance and forgiveness for their souls through the manifestation of the divine compassion and grace through that which Jesus was in his own soul and revealed in life and death, and have recognized that their need is the need of all men everywhere in every age, have recognized him as the Saviour of the world. This is not theology; it is experience. My 'argument' hitherto has been, as I believe, a demonstration that with complete intellectual honesty we may be open to what Jesus has to say to us about ourselves and God. It requires no little courage to be intellectually honest with ourselves. I can only say now with the apostle Paul, 'I beg you, in Christ's name, be reconciled to God' (II Cor. 5.20).

Many would willingly believe that God is love but cannot reconcile such a faith with the pain and evil of the world or even their own sufferings. I will come to that issue in the

[1] John Knox, *The Death of Christ* (Collins, 1959), esp. pp. 142. 144, 149 f., 152-156.

next chapter. I would deal first with the theological implications of that which I have just expounded.

The Gospel is that 'God so loved the world that he sent his Son' (John 3.16). I have put that in other terms: Jesus taught not merely the divine good will towards all men but also the divine initiative in their salvation. This good will and initiative was not merely his teaching, it was his life; he incarnated that which he taught, he made it credible because he showed it. It is not really sensible to suppose that God created a person better than himself! Moreover, we can see that if God was to make known to man a love boundless and to the uttermost, there was no means whereby this could be made credible to man unless it were shown in flesh and blood upon the stage of history. There is a logic in the Gospel.

I come now to what I may call the simplification of theology. There will be those Christians who will think ill of me for my critical or destructive criticism of traditional Christian theology. 'No one,' said William Windham, 'would select the hurricane season in which to begin repairing his house.' This certainly is the hurricane season for the Christian Church; it blows with fury from the steppes of Russia. But what is one to do if the house is already tumbling down? I have called my book a religion for agnostics. If traditional Christians like to say that this religion is not Christianity, I am unconcerned. It rests upon the simple facts of Jesus, but I must relate and connect religion as I understand it to that which the agnostic, not altogether incorrectly, supposes to be the religion of the churches.

This principle of the divine compassion made credible in Jesus is relevant to all religions. It does not render Christianity as we know it 'the true religion' nor render all other religion false. Much in church history and in current conventional Christianity is quite incompatible with the belief in the out-flowing, unquenchable grace of God. There are Christians, there are Hindus, there are Buddhists, there are Muslims, there are Jews on the other hand who, consciously or unconsciously, manifest much of the Spirit of Jesus in their lives. I should say of them, not that their professed religion is true, but that they have true religion. Many who call themselves agnostics or, it may be, even atheists show the marks of true religion in their lives, though they have no assurance of it in their minds. Let us be done with labels and look at realities alone. I conceive that the lives that such people lead find justification in that spiritual reality which was incarnate in the Man of Nazareth.

I might put the same point from another angle. Christian missions seek to convert the world to Christianity. Well and good. But what in fact they have incidentally or directly sought to do is to convert religious men of other religions to Methodism or Roman Catholicism or Presbyterianism or some other variety of Western religious culture. That is neither well nor good. To preach 'Christianity' is one thing, to tell the story of Jesus is another. I am, I hope, a Christian, but it is sadly clear to me that 'Christianity', while it proclaims Jesus, also hides him from the modern world.

I must relate what I am stumbling to say to the traditional doctrines proclaimed by Christianity. I start from what are usually regarded as the three fundamental doctrines of Christianity, the Trinity, the Divinity of Christ and the Atonement. All of these spring ultimately from that overwhelming religious conviction which inspired the early Church that had known Jesus and was assured of his vindication by the act of God. They are attempts to express the truth, but as attempts in the modern world they are for the most part unsuccessful.

I have elaborated elsewhere and need not here repeat

my conviction that the doctrine of the Trinity today normally regarded as orthodox is not merely unintelligible to all except specialists but even so is a great confusion. There are in fact several quite different doctrines of the Trinity, all of which are entirely 'orthodox', and all of which (even including the rather forbidding 'Athanasian Creed') come down to this, that God is personal and God is love.[1] Metaphysical theories about the Being of the incomprehensible God must be unsatisfactory or worse. If, as the years pass, we find an ever greater wealth of meaning in the familiar phrases, 'the grace of our Lord Jesus Christ', 'the love of God' and 'the fellowship of the holy Spirit' (about which I will say somewhat later), we need not be greatly concerned about orthodoxies or unorthodoxies of theological speculation. Apart from a growing understanding of these phrases there is no virtue in any of the speculations.

Let me turn aside for a paragraph to utter a warning against this word 'orthodoxy' which has seemed so all-important to many ecclesiastically minded persons. 'Orthodoxy' properly means correct opinion, and none of us has, or can have, a correct opinion about the mysterious and incomprehensible Being of the most high God. I will venture here to quote with great satisfaction from Dr Elmslie's address at Westminster College, Cambridge, on Commemoration Day 1959. He cites the text, 'By this shall all men know that you are my disciples, if you have love one to another' (John 13.35). He comments: 'Throughout the centuries those who have so loved Jesus that they loved their brethren have borne effective witness to Christ and his faith in God. On the other hand, how vast the tragedy that the organized churches in various ways have insisted that much else is *indispensable*; and each demanding the totality of its view has cried to the others Heretic! Heretic!—with

[1] *Faith and Reason* (Duckworth, 1963), pp. 102 ff.

the consequence that Christianity has floundered in miasmic swamps of cruelties and all uncharitableness. I assure you it is unconvincing to stigmatize as heretics those who give cold water to thirsting lips.'

The various doctrines of the 'divinity' of Jesus have been bold and honourable attempts by Christian thinkers to evaluate the significance of his person. Unfortunately they have had the effect of making him an unreal person to Christians and a figure of mythology or phantasy to those outside the Christian fold. It is inconceivable that Jesus should ever have required or willingly allowed any one to accept a doctrine of his own divinity. There is, however, in the Fourth Gospel a story which, not being 'out of character', may be a genuine reminiscence (John 14.8 ff.). Jesus had spoken much about 'the Father', and Philip is said to have urged him (I am not quite clear what Philip meant), 'Shew us the Father, and we shall be content.' To this Jesus replies, 'Have I been so long with you, Philip, and you have not known me? He who has seen me has seen the Father. How is it that you say, "Shew us the Father"? Do you not believe that I am in the Father, and the Father is in me? The words that I say to you I do not speak of myself; it is the Father abiding in me who performs his works.' This is as much as to say, 'The Son says nothing but what he hears the Father say,' just as in another place Jesus is reported to have said, 'The Son does nothing but what he sees the Father do' (John 5.19). We cannot be certain of the authenticity of these sayings, but they authentically reproduce the impression Jesus made upon those responsive to him; his words and deeds were the words and deeds of God. This, as the bringer of the kingdom, he claimed, but for himself he made no claim. To use modern psychological terms, we are dealing here with his God-consciousness, not his self-consciousness. He above and beyond all others 'denied himself', that is, he never thought about himself, his meat and drink being to do the will of God and to manifest his grace.

Yet we must attempt to answer the question expressed in such odd grammatical form in our Authorized Version, 'Whom say ye that I am?' The Fourth Gospel opens with the words: 'In the beginning was the Word.' We may paraphrase this by saying that in the beginning (whatever that means) was the Thought, the Purpose, the Plan of God. That, if there be a God, is a necessary and intelligible idea. St Augustine, who was steeped in the Platonic tradition, takes up this point and quotes further: in the beginning was the Word or Thought of God; the Word was with God and the Word was God (for the Thought is not to be separated from the Thinker); all creation comes from the Thought or Word or Plan of God, and apart from the Word was not anything made that was made. All this, says St Augustine, he read in the books of the philosophers. Indeed, we may say that, if there be a God, it stands to reason. But what the philosophers did not know and could not tell him, St Augustine continues, is that the Word became flesh and dwelt amongst us and we beheld his glory.

Let me put this in simple and more modern terms. The universal evolutionary order proceeds from the mind or purpose or will of God. It expresses his mysterious will and purpose. Man, when he arises in the course of this evolutionary process, is aware of a new spiritual environment or dimension unknown to lower forms of creation. Glimpses and intimations of this spiritual environment have been granted to poets, sages, prophets, artists and perhaps to all men everywhere. But truly 'Thou art a God that hidest thyself (Isa. 45.15); 'Clouds and darkness are round about him' (Ps. 97.2). The mind and purpose of God, the very heart of God, in relation to man, was declared and made known and incarnated in Jesus; he was in that sense God manifest in the flesh, in an historic human person. That, however mysterious, is intelligible; it makes sense; and it exactly corresponds to the apprehension of those who through the person of Jesus have believed in the love of God and have spiritually come home to God. This is not a metaphysical theory of the 'divinity' of Jesus but an attempt to state his significance in the spiritual history of man.

We have already trenched on the Atonement, which properly means at-one-ment. Through the divine initiative made known in the ministry and pre-eminently in the voluntary death of Jesus vindicating the infinite compassion and love of God for men the lost sheep is found, the prodigal son comes home and finds himself forgiven.

That is the essence of the matter. The theologies of the Atonement have been expressed in forms that no longer have any meaning for us, as a debt paid to the devil, as a mysterious transaction between the first and the second Persons of the Trinity, as the payment of a debt owed to God as if he were a feudal overlord, as an expiatory sacrifice. We cannot accept these theories but need not be scornful of them; they expressed for their day that which had to be expressed.

One comment only I would make. The New Testament, the traditional Christian liturgies, the language of evangelical religion are steeped in the idea of sacrifice. The modern man who has not been brought up in the *milieu* of traditional Christianity is puzzled, offended and totally unimpressed by the statement familiar on the lips of Christians that our sins are forgiven, and we are saved, 'by the blood of Jesus'. He sees no imaginable connection between any sins of which he may be conscious and an event that happened about two millennia ago, and in any case the

124

idea of redemption by blood seems to him to belong to the world of primitive religion. He pictures some god who needs to be propitiated by sacrifice and is ultimately and finally satisfied by the human self-sacrifice of Jesus. We do well to reject such ideas as these. But in fact we are somewhat unfair in ascribing such crudities to the New Testament. We still speak of life-blood; in Hebrew thought the life of an animal or man was located in his blood. When the priest in the old rituals sprinkled the blood of the slain animal on the altar or upon the worshippers, he was deemed to be dispensing the life of the sacrificial victim. This phrase 'the blood of Jesus' is a compendious, shorthand or technical phrase which written out in full would be represented by 'the life of Jesus who has passed through death'. 'We are saved by his *life*', says the apostle Paul (Rom. 5.10).

Let me sum up the argument of the preceding pages. I am presuming to suggest a religion for agnostics, by whom I mean in particular those who are not irreligious but are both puzzled and offended by the claim of the Christian religion to be the true religion over against all false religions, to be final, and to be expressed and accepted in terms of traditional doctrine.

First, then, I should not say that 'Christianity' is the true religion and all others are false, for if Jesus in his relationship to God and his neighbour was the truly religious man, then much of actual and historical 'Christianity' is not true religion at all. If the man who makes this claim protests, 'of course I mean that *real* Christianity is the true religion', he is saying no more than that real religion, the religion of Jesus, is true religion, which is very different from the assertion that what the world knows as 'Christianity' is alone the true religion.

Never did Jesus call upon his contemporaries to abandon

Judaism and adopt a new religion; he did not set himself to found 'a new religion'; he recalled men to God whom they mistrusted, misunderstood and grievously misrepresented. The earliest Christians did not cease to be, and regarded themselves as, Jews; we read that they worshipped daily in the Temple (Acts 2.46). Christian missionaries to Islam have invited and exhorted Muslims to abandon their religion and become Presbyterians or Anglicans or Roman Catholics instead. I dream that they might have said, 'Be loyal to your religious vision in Islam but take seriously, as you have not yet, the fact and figure of Jesus of Nazareth.' I can see that the preaching of Jesus (not 'the Christian religion') to an Islam bound to the letter of the Koran might have as disturbing and revolutionary an effect as was the word of Jesus to a Judaism bound to the letter of the Law. But in Islam now, as in Jewry then, there are many whose minds and hearts are open. I know there are Christians who think we must preach not only Christ but the Church also with its recognized and official ministries as part of 'Christ'. I do not think the Church unimportant, but I see no justification for this view in the Gospels.

The claim of Christianity to finality is a further stumbling block. I think this need not trouble us. I am sure that the religion of the future, the common religion which will attract all mankind, will be very different from the Christianity of history. There is nothing final about Christian doctrines and Christian institutions, but, on the principle that no angle can be more right than a right angle, I am content to say that if the attitude of Jesus to God his Father and to man his brother was right, there cannot be an attitude more right; we have therefore the same kind of finality that for geometricians attaches to a right angle.

The traditional Christian doctrines are not final; they need to be radically revised if the truth to which they point is to be made intelligible today. If one has come to believe that God is he from whom, through whom and in whom are all things, that his infinite compassion and outgoing grace to man is incarnated in Jesus, and that Jesus reconciles or at-ones us with God, giving us peace and joy and assurance and hope, one has apprehended, as I suppose, the religious intuition which lies behind the traditional doctrines which are outgrown.

10

PAIN, SIN AND DEATH

'WE should like to believe that God is love,' men say, 'but all the evil and suffering in the world since the beginning of time are incompatible with the existence of such a Being.' About this I would make two initial comments: first, the existence of evil, of so much evil, in the world remains to the end of argument a baffling and insoluble enigma; second, the presence of this enigma in the world must not be made an excuse, as it so often is, for refusing to face the implications of our moral certainties.

On the one hand, we cannot understand all this suffering; on the other, we cannot reasonably suppose that Jesus is more patient, more forgiving and more loving than his heavenly Father. What should we say of a man of science who, having discovered some new fact, should say, 'This fact is incompatible with other well-established facts; therefore I will not believe what I have discovered'? We should say he was being intellectually and morally dishonest. His duty as a scientist is to deny neither the fact he had discovered nor the facts previously known but rather to reconsider accepted knowledge in the light of this new fact.

I propose, then, briefly and most inadequately to look at the problem of evil and suffering in the light of the revelation of the love of God incarnate in the Christ. I can only offer pointers, not a theory. In the teaching of Jesus we find no theory; he accepted the current phraseology which spoke of the present period as the age or realm of Satan to be displaced in God's good time by the kingdom or realm or age of God. We may confidently say of Jesus that he was much more sensitive to, and constantly aware of, the sufferings of men than we; his life was given to destroying 'the works of the devil'; but none was ever so serenely conscious of the love of God as he.

Suffering is a very private matter. We can infer, and we must try to imagine and alleviate, other people's sufferings, but we only know our own. We must not treat suffering as if it were a quantity; we must not mentally pile up all the sufferings of mankind since the beginning of time, all the hunger, cruelty, oppressions, slavery, wars, massacres and diseases into some imaginary Everest of suffering, and ask how a loving God could be responsible for that. The wise plan will be to begin with our own suffering which alone we know and ask ourselves whether we can regard that as incompatible with the divine compassion. We may, I think, apply to suffering that which J. M. Creed wrote about sin. 'Sin', he said, 'as a mere fact outside oneself may seem to constitute a serious objection to belief in a Providential ordering of the world, but actual consciousness of sin will always afford the surest approach to belief in God and the chief clue to the Christian confession of the divinity of Jesus Christ.'[1]

There is, I think, an almost morbid element in modern thought upon this subject. Our spiritual fathers thought of this earth as 'a vale of tears', of life as a stern discipline, of preparation for death as the great task of life. Here too, it may be, there was a morbid element, though we should remember that they lived before the day of anaesthetics. But we think of life, or tend to think of it, in terms of 'having a good time', of raising our 'standard of living';

[1] J. M. Creed, *The Divinity of Jesus Christ* (Fontana ed., 1964), pp. 139 f.

we are apt to be resentful of suffering when it comes to us as if we were ill-used by Providence.

I judge that it would be morbid to desire suffering and to seek for it, but if suffering comes, as it does to all of us, in the way of duty or of circumstance, we must accept it. Some men, when suffering comes, are made resentful, embittered, hardened by it; others are patient, becoming softened, made more understanding, more gentle, more useful, more sympathetic by it. All depends upon the spirit in which suffering is taken. It was said of Jesus that 'he learnt by the things that he suffered' (Heb. 5.8). Most of us would say that we have learnt more and grown more through days of suffering than in sunnier days. Suffering is not of itself an evil unless we resent it, and in that case it is the resentment rather than the suffering that is the evil. As I walk in the streets I see in the faces of old people, especially of women and of poor people, the marks of suffering, patience, endurance, courage, a spiritual beauty. In the biographies of those of noble character I like to observe the portraits of the subject, as a child, as a young man, in middle life, in old age. What marks of splendour and of suffering, of splendour attained through suffering! One Sunday evening long ago John Kelman of Free St George's Edinburgh, read aloud to a group of students the whole of Coulson Kernahan's short book, *The Man of No Sorrows*. In detail I forget it all, but I remember that it depicted an imaginary figure endowed with every grace of form, of intellect, of health, of skill, of power, a benevolent dictator, the benefactor of mankind, providing 'bread and circuses' for all. The expressed or implicit moral of the book was not to be escaped. Such a figure was not comparable in grandeur or in glory to the Man of Sorrows out of Galilee. Suffering is not in itself incompatible with the grace and love of God.

It is, I suppose, probable that sensitivity to pain increases with the development of nervous sensibility. As we learn 'the laws of nature', we learn increasingly to deal with pain. There is a touching and often repeated prayer before the days of anaesthetics, '. . . and suffer us not, O Lord, through any pains of death to fall from thee.' The pains of death have been mercifully alleviated in these days for those in touch with modern medicine. I suppose that the development of nervous sensibility which increases our sensitivity to pain increases at the same time our sensitivity to beauty. In moments of mental stress we may be tempted to envy the cows that crop the grass so placidly with no present problems and no eerie future to trouble their contented spirits, but this is a mood to which we may not give way. Better than to be a cow is to glory in the beauty of the sunlit fields and to bear the burdens of our neighbours!

We are apt to distinguish mental pain from physical, though in fact all pain is of the mind or mental. Our mental hospitals are sadly full; the waiting-rooms of psychiatric doctors, I am told, are crowded; to become civilized, it seems, is to become neurotic. Gastric ulcers, nervous breakdowns, periods in mental hospitals and suicides are the commonplaces of our urban, industrial and mercantile society. We are a maladjusted generation, maladjusted to life, to our duties, to our neighbours, to our God. It is significant, and too little observed, that Jesus who bore on his heart, as no other, the sorrows and burdens of mankind showed no signs of nervous breakdown but was serene through all the storms that raged around him.

But what of 'evil' and suffering in Nature, below the level of human life? Our thinking has been much bedevilled by Tennyson's often quoted description of 'Nature red in tooth and claw', as if the animal kingdom were one vast

131

bloody battlefield. It is true, of course, that all creatures prey upon one another, nor is the strictest vegetarian amongst us in reality exempt from this necessity. The 'psychology' of other creatures is hidden from us, but from their conduct and behaviour it would appear that the life of birds, animals and fish is not unhappy. Suicide is almost unknown amongst them! They have their moments of terror and of pain, but normally these are short, and death comes quickly. We can see, too, or think that we can see, that without some stimulus of fear and pain the marvellous skills and beauties of the animal creation, the cunning of the lapwing, the fleetness of the roe, could never have been developed. Moreover, if all creatures, like us men in this, neither live unto themselves nor die unto themselves, nothing is here incompatible with the love of God. Mystery, indeed, remains, but we tend to make too much of suffering in nature.

But apart from the sufferings of animals there is evil, men say, in the remorseless operation of the laws of nature. How many sailors has the cruel sea submerged, how many villages, towns and cities have been laid waste by earthquake, avalanche, flood and pestilence! How could these things be if God were good?

We ask our indignant question in the dark. Self-preservation is a natural instinct. We are apt to suppose, but have no sufficient reason for supposing, that death is an evil and a disaster for the one who dies. 'Poor fellow,' we say, 'he was drowned at sea!' But how do we know that he needs our pity and commiseration? What death is, no man living knows. It is well that we reckon with our ignorance.

But, apart from death, what suffering has been caused, and is caused today, by eruptions, earthquakes, famines, hurricanes and floods! These disasters were called in old days 'visitations', as if God in his inscrutable wisdom thought fit to inflict these miseries on selected victims. Science and piety or reverence combine to forbid our thinking in such terms today. It ill befits us to be resentful of those violent convulsions in virtue of which our habitable earth was formed! We should not ask that the laws of nature be suspended now that man has appeared on earth. We must neither be callous nor sentimental. All suffering is private; suffering is not intrinsically and of itself an evil, as we ought to know from our own experience. It is required of us that we hasten to the relief of distress as we are able. When we see it, we often become aware of the love, the patience, the courage, the magnificence which it evokes. Furthermore, we must not claim to know why the universe is not other than it is; we are learning to deal with flood and famine and disease; this is part of the great and tragic and glorious story of humanity. What a paradox it is! We are bound to prevent and alleviate suffering wherever that lies within our power. But suppose, for a moment, that after some generations by the wisdom of science and the skill of technology we could eradicate flood, famine and disease from all the world (and simultaneously achieve a manageable and rational population of the earth), is it quite certain that this would be a better world than that in which we live? How little do we really know! It is obvious that we must seek to alleviate suffering wherever possible; it is very far from obvious that the world's suffering is incompatible with God's love.

Here I must turn aside for a moment to consider a question that greatly troubles many religious men. Is it, then, both useless and superstitious to pray for deliverance from storms at sea or disasters upon land? Does God never 'interfere' with the course of nature? According to our present state of knowledge the answer, I am sure, must be that God never 'interferes' in the sense of acting directly apart from 'secondary causes'; that is to say, no event occurs of which ideally a proper scientific account cannot be given. But there is more to be said than that. His experience has led a well-known doctor to assert that patients who are prayed for by their friends are more likely to recover than other patients in a similar condition. If this principle be true, as it may be, we shall have to say that prayer is one of the causes that operate in nature, and this will then be a scientific fact. The truth is that we do not know and cannot imagine in what way the universe is related to the Being in whom and for whom it has existence. On the one hand, we must say that God does not 'interfere' with the order of the world; on the other hand, we now know that the universe is not a vast mechanism rigidly determined; the unexpected, the unpredictable occurs; the Power transcendent over nature is also immanent within it. How can God influence the course of events without interfering with the laws of nature? That God does not 'interfere' we may be said to know; but not less clear is it that the course of Evolution, as we can trace it, shows the marks of a Power and a Guidance bringing order out of chaos, man from matter. I often ponder the suggestion of an earlier theologian that the relation of the world to God may best be compared to the relation of a child in the womb to the mother who is bearing it. To believe in the efficacy of prayer is not unscientific.

Pain and suffering, for all our explanations, must remain a mystery beyond our present solving, but we should not speak of evil in nature, for evil is a moral term.

Why should there be moral evil if God is good? Various mythological answers have been offered such as the pre-mundane fall of the angels or Adam's transgression at the beginning of the world. But we can see that if there was to be moral good, there must have been moral evil. If we could not deliberately do good, the attainment of character, the realization of our humanity, would be impossible; but if we must be able deliberately to do good, we must necessarily be able equally to do evil. Why do we in fact from time to time deliberately choose evil? The answer, I think, is that we never deliberately choose evil. As the philosophers say, we can only desire the good. That is, the only motive for action is the desire of some good. That which we desire may in itself be an evil, such as the extra slice of cake that will give us indigestion or the extra finger of whisky which will qualify our skill upon the roads, but we only take these indulgences because at the moment they seem to us desirable and good: 'When the woman saw that the tree was good for food, and that it was pleasant to the eyes, and a tree to be desired to make one wise, she took of the fruit thereof, and did eat, and gave also to her husband with her; and he did eat' (Gen. 3.6).

Yes, but Adam and Eve in the legend knew quite well that they were doing wrong. Why should we all do wrong, as we all do? If I steal today (stealing, I may say, is not one of the evils to which I am specially addicted), it is because of the kind of person I am, and the kind of person I am today depends upon the kind of person I was yesterday, and I was that kind of person because of the kind of person I was the day before, and so backwards to the very first time when I stole something as a child (though in fact I think I never did). Why did I make my first wrong choice and deliberately do evil? There is, I judge, a real mystery here but not such that about it we can say nothing. If we are to learn to be persons, we must assert ourselves against our surroundings and the world about us, including the conventions laid upon us. Because of our ignorance as children it is impossible we should know by instinct what are the right and what the wrong forms of self-assertion;

this we can only learn, and fortunate are we if we have a home and surroundings in which it is easy for us to learn where to assert ourselves and where to restrain our appetites. I doubt whether we need any theory of 'original sin' and of a taint in human nature. Mistaken choices are inevitable if we are to learn, and what we have to learn is that which is most desirable and wherein we can come to be that which we ought and desire to be.

Sin, therefore, if we care to use that word, is inevitable and not incompatible with God's goodness. But this, it may be said, is a formal argument and fails to meet the objection that the results of sin are the broken homes, the cruelty to children, the wars, the massacres, the tortures, the oppressions and the appalling tale of suffering which is one aspect, and not the least obvious, in the story of humanity. This difficulty must be faced, and, once again, no logically satisfying answer is available. Enough if in the darkness of a great mystery we can apprehend that human suffering through the ages may not be incompatible with the love of God as shown in the life and death of Jesus.

If we were merely individuals and not persons, there would be no answer. Why should others be allowed to inflict suffering and misery on their fellows? But we are not mere individuals; we are so constituted that we belong to one another, that we do not even exist as persons out of relation to other people. Before we were born, our relation to our mothers was most intimate. At birth we have to learn to be members of a family. Then we must learn to accommodate ourselves to a wider fellowship. This may be conveniently illustrated by the vivid history of Scotland where there first developed the wonderful unity and loyalty of the clan; therein men learnt to live together in a unity both close and terrible; later came the unity of the nation largely based upon a common hatred of the English. Then the Scots and the English so learnt to live together as a wider nation that today the past seems almost inconceivable to us. Then the Scots with the English were called to look for a wider common life in the service of that empire which, when I was young, covered so vast a portion of the habitable earth. The empire has passed away leaving some trail of glory and of splendour in spite of all our failures now so manifest. All the world is in turmoil at this time; nationalisms, revolutions, civil wars, and terrors and horrors are the daily diet of our newspapers. It will be generations or centuries before all the peoples of the earth, doubtless through great suffering, come to live in harmony with one another, but to this new and better world-order we are all inexorably being driven, God having prepared for some future generation (to use biblical language) some better thing which we now shall not live here to see.

If we think of the sufferings of this present time and the prolonged and terrible sufferings of times past as a vast mass and mountain of suffering, we cannot say that all this is justified by the felicity of some future generation; but this is to treat suffering as a measurable quantity. All men suffer and some suffer terribly. Is it in vain? Does it lead to nothing? Many have been broken by it, but what magnificence of character, what heroism, what patience, what sympathy, what love it has evoked! One day, I suppose, we shall conquer cancer as we have conquered leprosy and diabetes. Those who have suffered and died from these diseases have really suffered and died that others might be saved from them. It is not in war only, it is the common lot of life that men and women die for one another. That the sufferings of Jesus have brought immeasurable good to man we all can see. We should not think it a fairer world were it not for the Man of Sorrows. Would it be a fairer world in which men and women did not suffer and die

137

for one another? It may be said that Jesus suffered willingly and open-eyed, but most suffer unwillingly and blindly. Yes, but we do not know the story's end. We do not know the story's end either for mankind as a whole or for any individual in it.

There is a saying of Joubert, *'Souffrir passe; avoir suffré ne passe jamais.'* We cannot profitably discuss man's pains and sufferings without considering whether this transitory life is all that he will know. There are many who suppose that when we die the self of which we are conscious disappears like a candle flame when it is blown out. Science can neither prove this nor disprove it. The Hebrews in biblical times thought of man as an animated body; the philosophical Greeks, on the other hand, thought of him as a spirit encaged in a body. It is the Greek idea that was generally adopted by the Christians, who found it easy to suppose that at death the spirit flies away in freedom being no longer tied to a perishable and material body. We now better understand the intimate connection between the mental and the physical; we talk of psychosomatic symptoms. The psychiatrists are constantly busied with the physical afflictions due to mental maladjustments to life; the physicians ascribe temperamental differences and aberrations to glands instead of to the influence of the planets; they seek to cure mental afflictions by potions or shock treatments. A knock on the head or some other injury to the brain, we are told, can alter a man's character. The relation between the mental and the physical is so intimate that we are often told to dispense with the old idea of 'the soul' which can nowhere be located or discerned; we must deal with a psycho-physical whole which exists and then ceases to exist as a whole; there is no place for a soul that could outlive the physical organism which undoubtedly dies and decays.

The confusion here involved is due largely to the tendency, falsely regarded as scientific, to identify mind and brain. If I have forgotten the name of someone I met last week I 'cudgel my brains' to remember. *I* cudgel my brains. The 'I' that cudgels is not to be identified with the recalcitrant instrument that is cudgelled. Again, I may see a golden object, I may hear the word 'gold' spoken in a deep bass voice, I may hear it spoken in a childish treble, I may read it in print, I may feel it in braille if I have learnt to read that way. In those cases my brain will have received five quite different impressions, but by some mysterious alchemy which we do not begin to understand the mind interprets all those different impressions by the common idea of 'gold'. The brain is undoubtedly the instrument of our thinking; it is the *instrument* of *our* thinking. The brain is a marvellously complicated engine; it needs exercise; we 'must use our brains'. What do we mean here by 'we'?

The word 'soul' has gone out of fashion, but the new word 'personality' has come into our language and our thought. We can only express ourselves through our bodies, but we must all be conscious from time to time that neither words nor deeds can manage to convey all that is in our hearts. We are so much more than ever we manage to express, and most of us are very inarticulate about our deepest feelings, our sublimest insights. Our bodies and brains fail us here, and sometimes our bodies fail us altogether, and our real self is almost wholly concealed as when the brain gives way and we are certified as mad. A great biography, an intimate journal or a volume of poems may make us feel that the subject was so much more than we ever realized or he could fully say. By what used to be called the soul I mean that character, that person, the subject of infinite longings and unmeasurable affections and

139

flashing insights never fully expressed or even expressible. This character or person is indeed at the moment united with a physical body but is itself a spiritual, not a physical or material, thing. As it grows older the body may fail it more and more, but there is no compelling reason to suppose that this spiritual thing ceases to exist when its body perishes.

The Psychical Research Society can offer some not unimpressive but not altogether convincing evidence of survival after death. When our friends die, it would be pleasant to be able to think that we shall see them again one day, but I doubt whether that abstraction known as 'the modern man' really desires that immortality in which so many have believed in previous generations. Many think that there may be a hereafter, and, the fear of hell having wholly departed, they hope that the next life, if there be one, will prove rather better than the present. What would 'rather better' mean if it were not in terms of a larger pay-packet, longer holidays, no taxes and television in super-glorious technicolor? This at least would seem to most a more alluring prospect than heaven as it has been traditionally depicted by Christians in terms of permanent residence in church under conditions particularly trying to those who are unmusical.

'The world as known to us remains a broken unintelligible fragment which to the end leaves man questioning and unsatisfied.'[1] The pains and sufferings of unnumbered generations cannot be mentally reconciled with the idea of the Fatherhood of God, as Jesus taught it, if this life on earth be all. We cannot prove a future life, and it is doubtful how far the modern man desires it. On the other hand, I think we may say that the human race would long ago have perished by mutual destruction if God or History or

[1] J. M. Creed, *The Divinity of Jesus Christ*, p. 20.

Providence were not always bringing good out of evil. Of this principle the death of Jesus is the supreme example.

Has our human life any ultimate significance? Or is it but a multicoloured bubble that bursts when we go down to death? I will recount a dream. I cannot in any degree picture a life beyond death which is presumably an existence no longer under the conditions of time and space. Therefore I dream that at death the scales fall from the eyes of the soul or person or character or individual ego, the subject of love and sorrow and frustration and joy and suffering on earth, and it sees the truth about itself and its earthly life at last. Or, to put the matter more concretely, I dream that the soul or personality awakes to the conscious presence of Jesus who was the incarnation of truth about human life. I dream that those who have deliberately exercised cruelty upon their fellows on a large scale or a small will realize at last what they have done: 'they shall see him whom they have pierced', and what Scripture calls 'the pains of hell' will get hold upon them till they are remade; and I dream that the sufferers of humanity, the slaves, the oppressed, those who have suffered in their bodies or in their hearts so grievously, will become aware of the divine compassion and will see how their sufferings like the sufferings of the Christ have contributed to that consummation of all things which we now cannot even envisage, and that seeing what has been wrought through their sufferings they will find in them nothing inconsistent with the eternal love of God. That is a dream, but it might come true—or something very like it; indeed, that or something like it must come true, for otherwise not only is human life meaningless, which we cannot easily believe; but we should have to deny our deepest assurances and intuitions which centre round the Man of Nazareth.

I come to a final point where our mortal vision fades.

Love means sympathy, and sympathy means suffering. If that be so, how can we think of God as loving? It is only by a violent anthropomorphism that we picture God as suffering. In sermons we are sometimes told that God wishes for something that he has not, God attempts something which he does not achieve, God is glad or God is sad. It is perhaps not possible in popular exposition to avoid language of this kind, but it is unpleasing, almost blasphemous in the ears of those who have some sense of the eternal majesty, the ineffable Being whom we so dimly apprehend. We seem almost on the horns of this dilemma: if God does not suffer, he does not love; if God suffers, he is not God. It is well here to recollect the saying of the epistle to the Hebrews (12.2) that Jesus 'for the joy that was set before him' endured the Cross. Elsewhere Scripture points to the mother who forgets her pains in the joy that a man-child is born to her (John 16.21). We cannot escape from our dilemma, but we can dimly conceive how the passion of the world is taken up into the beatitude of God, if we believe that death is not the end, and the purposes of God are yet to be fulfilled in joy.

11

THE WORLD IN WHICH I LIVE

As I admitted in my preface I do not in fact derive the beliefs by which I live from the argument I have adduced. My argument, therefore, may be called a 'rationalization', to use the jargon of the psychologists, but it has been an honest argument, and to me it is important. Where in the dark we cannot see our way, we must be guided by instinct or intuition and by such stars as can be discerned. In matters of the spirit we cannot possess truth so as to systematize or manipulate it. In that sense we must remain agnostic, but I believe that truth may possess us if we are open to it. I accept the old distinction between that reason which is 'discursive' and that which is 'intuitive'. By discursive reason I understand the scientific or logical process which moves from point to point and ends in demonstration, but there is, said the ancient philosopher Proclus, a perception of the spirit or the soul. This is the sphere of the intuitive reason, to which, as we are seekers after truth, the name of reason must not be denied. If anyone of my friends says to me that for himself he is quite unaware of any spiritual world, there is no argument by which I can confute him, but I do not quite believe him. I know he is telling me what he believes about himself, but I look also at what he does, the way he conducts his life, the assurances and principles by which he stands. Then he appears to me 'like one whose untried ear a murmuring stream detains'. I notice how kind and generous he is, how he trusts his wife, how limitless is his affection for his children; I observe his reverence for goodness and heroic action and, indeed, for every kind of excellence. He walks in fact by faith, but a not unreasonable faith. I believe that he is right to trust that faith by which he lives, and that he should accept the intellectual implications of it.

My argument, I have said, is important to myself; it is, indeed, an argument conducted with myself, for I know both lassitude and torpor of spirit and have constant occasion to wrestle with the spectres of the mind and spirit. Intellectual integrity is demanded of us; we must away with superstition, whether it be scientific or religious superstition; we may not interpret life according to our wishes in mere self-deception, but we must be loyal to all those assurances which we cannot deny without intellectual or spiritual dishonour. I am quite persuaded that between Science and Religion there is no such incompatibility of nature or of temperament as should be just cause or impediment to prevent a fruitful marriage. I accept with my reason, and make no attempt to prove, that it is reasonable and required of us that we seek to acquire those graces and that character which men call civilized or humane, the proper flowering of humanity. But a far greater challenge to my reason and personal integrity is this figure of Jesus Christ whom I can for a time avoid but not in the end evade. Much mythology gathers around his figure, but he is, as seems to me certain, a figure of history, not of imagination and mythology; the main outline of his life, his character, his teaching and his death are clear enough. He was a great ethical teacher, but with that I am not most concerned; the vital question, that affects my whole outlook upon life, is whether in respect of that Beyond which is hidden from our mortal sight he was at once the great deceiver and the great deceived, or whether in his own person he represents the way, the truth, the life. In other words, is that boundless compassion towards the suffering and sinful of mankind based on the most glorious and pitiful illusion known to history, or is it a revelation of the divine? I recall that if God be like that, there is no other way in which that truth could be revealed or made credible than in a human being who incarnated and manifested it through all that suffering or sin could inflict upon him. Am I to think of Jesus as a glorious and pitiful freak in an unintelligible drama of Evolution, or is he the key to the agelong process? It is to me a matter of intellectual and personal integrity to believe that he spoke truly and was true; I must take the consequences of this belief.

The consequences involve, of course, a great stimulus to ethical and personal endeavour, a permanent and utter self-dissatisfaction or, to use the traditional language of theology, a sense of sin, but that is a private matter not for public exposition. I have called this chapter 'the world in which I live', not because my way of life is a proper example to any one but because I think I now understand what the apostle meant when he wrote, 'The life I now live, I live by faith in the Son of God who loved me and gave himself for me' (Gal. 2.20). My spirit is very well aware of

> Her vassalage that binds her to the earth,
> Her sad dependence upon time, and all
> The trepidations of mortality.

Like everybody else I lead an ordinary life, eating, sleeping, talking, shopping, joking, reading, playing; but, real as this life is, it has for me more and more a dreamlike quality. My underneath or real life seems to me to be found in those moments when, like the flying fish emerging into the sunshine, I breathe for a while another air and see a new horizon. I am far from being always conscious of that of which I am aware when, as I suppose, I am most myself.

C. S. Lewis has explained from his own experience how simultaneously one can live two lives. He describes how the title of the book, *Siegfried and the Twilight of the Gods,* with Rackham's illustrations, broke upon his consciousness with an immense excitement and awakening. 'From that first moment in the schoolroom at Chartres', he writes, 'my secret, imaginative life began to be so important and so distinct from my outer life that I almost have to tell two separate stories. The two lives do not seem to influence one another at all. Where there are hungry wastes, starving for Joy, in the one, the other may be full of cheerful bustle and success; or again, where the outer life is miserable, the other may be brimming over with ecstasy. By the imaginative life I here mean only my life as concerned with Joy.[1] It should be remembered that Lewis uses 'Joy' in a rather special sense; he distinguishes it from pleasure, even from aesthetic pleasure: 'it must have the stab, the pang, the inconsolable longing'. Of Joy he says: 'it is never a possession, always a desire for something longer ago or further away or still about to be.' So the poet Meyerstein could write:

> The outer of the writer's mind was sad,
> But held a secret hearth of fiery glee.

I think that Lewis's Joy is that which I have tried to express in terms of a sense of the Presence or of the Infinite with the corresponding emotion of immeasurable thankfulness. We can and do live two lives, an inner and an outer, but in the passage I have quoted, Lewis so stresses the separateness of the two as to suggest what we now call schizophrenia, from which he did not suffer. I do not

[1] *Surprised by Joy,* p. 79.

146

think of the two worlds in which I live as separate in that way, the light of the infinite and the eternal is upon all the finite and the transient; the world of the Spirit impinges all the time upon our mortal spirits, but it is only at moments, rare moments perhaps at first, but more regular as one grows, that the soul of man is conscious of that infinite world about him, of which the finite is somehow the vehicle or signature.

I must start from my garden and the argument of my first chapters. The honeysuckle and the peonies are flowering now, and the poppies are untidy. All this I notice as I walk under the trees and hear the music of the insects and the birds and the rustling of the wind above me in the branches. Unnumbered sensations press upon my consciousness. But a sensation is meaningless; it is just a feeling. That which sensations awake in me is a sense of beauty and of wonder. The wonder lies partly in the ever-renewed mystery of life, the plants that survived the winter and now thrust out these incredible blossoms, the cherry trees that a week or two ago were one unbelievable glory of white blossom, the birds nesting and making love, the shy hedgehog emerging from his wintry sleep. I cannot see any reason for it all; it is wonder, it is mystery, it is beauty; it speaks to me, and I am utterly unable to explain to the reader or to myself precisely what it says. Its word may perhaps be somewhat expressed in negative as when Wordsworth speaks of

> such objects as excite
> No morbid passions, no disquietude,
> No vengeance and no hatred.

My apprehension is in terms of emotion, not of statement, by my interest is not in my emotions but in the birds, the flowers, the hedgehog and the trees. Why are they, what is the meaning of this annual, this perennial drama? Is there no meaning in it, is no purpose served? It is Nature, and I know and feel myself as part of Nature; I am one with the birds, the hedgehog and the flowers; yet I know them as they do not know me; I am full of wonder and am dazed with beauty. Then there are the books in my study which will tell me what the botanists and the ornithologists and the physicists have to say about it all. They increase my wonder but do nothing at all to elucidate the mystery. All this that I see and hear, as I gather, has evolved through immeasurable ages from some original whirling gases, some intricate and unimaginable strife or attraction of electrons which are just little energies, whatever that may mean. Indeed, if I may believe what I am told, the whole physical universe is a complicated system or series of constellations of these little energies; analyse to the end these leaves and blossoms, these little bodies and my own brain and you come to these ultimate units or 'particles' of energy. But this analysis is insufficient. From birds and flowers sound-waves and light-waves, so they tell me, strike upon my ears and eyes; these are waves of energy; from ears and eyes electric currents, another form of energy, run to my brain. But the music that I hear, the glory that I see is not an energy, or if it be an energy of my mind, then energy is something spiritual. Through these electric discharges and these 'waves' there is awakened in me a sense of wonder and of endless thankfulness. Thankfulness to What or Whom? Why did that Power which is the Energy, Origin of all energies, call into being these particular blossoms which when I look upon them seem so beautiful to me, or call into being the loves and songs of birds? I cannot tell. The information the books give me about all these objects cannot in any ultimate way explain them. All that I *know* about my garden is what it says to

148

me, and what it says cannot be set down in words. My mind is in some direct contact with the Power—'nearer is he than breathing, closer than hands and feet'.

What I am trying to say has been much better said by Wordsworth in the fourth book of *The Excursion*. One more quotation, an extended one this time, may be allowed me:

> I have seen
> A curious child, who dwelt upon a tract
> Of inland ground, applying to his ear
> The convolutions of a smooth-lipped shell;
> To which, in silence hushed, his very soul
> Listened intensely; and his countenance soon
> Brightened with joy; for murmurings from within
> Were heard, sonorous cadences! whereby
> To his belief, the monitor expressed
> Mysterious union with its native sea.
> Even such a shell the universe itself
> Is to the ear of faith; and there are times,
> I doubt not, when to you it doth impart
> Authentic tidings of invisible things;
> Of ebb and flow, and ever-during power;
> And central peace, subsisting in the heart
> Of endless agitation. Here you stand,
> Adore, and worship, when you know it not;
> Pious beyond the intention of your thought;
> Devout above the meaning of your will.
> Yes, you have felt, and may not cease to feel,
> The estate of man would be indeed forlorn
> If false conclusions of the reasoning power
> Made the eye blind, and closed the passages
> Through which the ear converses with the heart.
> Has not the soul, the being of your life,
> Received a shock of awful consciousness,

In some calm season, when these lofty rocks
At night's approach bring down the unclouded sky,
To rest upon their circumambient walls;
A temple framing of dimensions vast,
And yet not too enormous for the sound
Of human anthems,—choral song, or burst
Sublime of instrumental harmony,
To glorify the Eternal!

The theologians speak of Jesus of Nazareth as God in-carnate and sometimes of a *kenosis* or 'self-emptying' of God that he might appear in human guise (Phil. 2.7). I have explained why I hesitate to use these terms, but I will now adopt them to speak about my garden. I accept all that the physcists tell me about this rose that is break-ing into bud; it is a system and collocation of electrons, a form of complicated energy; but when I see the rose I am directly conscious of the Power; the rose to me is an incarnation of the Power, a very insufficient incarnation of the Power, no doubt; there has been a *kenosis* or self-emptying of the Power that is expressed in this rose-bud; it is a soundless unarticulated word of God to me; it points beyond itself to that which is beyond the grasp of human nature's Power. It is, I believe, an earnest or foretaste of the Word, that glory which I hope to know and experience hereafter. It points to the eternal glory.

That Word which Nature speaks is not to be set down in human language. The ultimate end and purpose of this vast evolutionary order is beyond imagining, but because through Jesus of Nazareth I have come to believe that compassion and joy are at the heart of the Eternal, I believe in consequence that it is love which moves the stars and directs the course of Nature, nor indeed would such beauty be compatible with anything but love and joy. That saint and scientist, Teilhard de Chardin, saw this far more clearly, felt it far more deeply than do I: *'Throughout* my life, *by means of* my life, the world has little by little caught fire in my sight, until, aflame all around me, it has become almost completely luminous from within . . . Such has been my experience in contact with the earth—the diaphany of the Divine at the heart of the universe on fire . . . Christ; his heart; a fire: capable of penetrating everywhere and, gradually, spreading everywhere.'[1]

It would, I think, be very rare to find an atheist amongst gardeners, agricultural workers, sailors such as the North Sea fishermen and the whalers, or among Bedouin travelling over the wastes by day and sleeping beneath the stars at night. Most in the Western world today live in conurbations which are as ugly as the name we give to them. They are surrounded all day by artefacts. Apart from an occasional stroll in the parks or glimpse of the sky between high buildings they are out of touch with Nature except human nature and greengroceries. This is an artificial and unnatural life or at least a life to which human nature is not really adapted. Urban man does not live under conditions which of themselves cause him to think of God. The 'secularism' and irreligion of today is connected very closely with the artificiality of urban life. I do not in the least mean that city dwellers cannot be religious, but unless they live near Kew or have weekend cottages in the country, they are deprived of a natural 'means of grace'.

But they are not deprived of people! I leave my garden, then, and contemplate my neighbours. My attitude to my neighbours is often very wrong; I am irritated by them, misjudge them, am put off by their manners, intensely dislike in them the qualities I so much dislike in myself, and am sometimes contemptuous of them, but never when I

[1] *Le Milieu Divin* (Fontana ed., 1964), p. 46 n.

151

stop to think. Jesus of Nazareth (and, of course, those who are like him) have taught me to see all human beings with new eyes and, I believe, to see them truly. I think of familiar lines from F. W. H. Myers's *St Paul*:

> Only as souls I see the folk thereunder,
>   Bound who should conquer, slaves who should be
>   kings,
> Hearing their one hope with an empty wonder,
>   Sadly contented with a show of things.

I hesitate to quote the stanza following:

> Then with a rush the intolerable craving
>   Shivers throughout me like a trumpet call,—
> Oh to save these! to perish for their saving,
>   Die for their life, be offered for them all!

St Paul might so speak, but it is not for me. I must write in an altogether lower key. I have often been shocked in hotels and shops at the way people are treating those who are serving them as if these servants were animated things, not persons. I am appalled by the way people can misunderstand one another, and intentionally or quite unintentionally be cruel to one another. When I stop to think, as I do not always stop to think, I am enabled to judge other people as I should wish to be judged myself. I am not sure whether to speak of compassion or sympathy or affection. I am certain that so to see people is to see them truly, and as a plain matter of history this outlook is derived from Jesus and none other. I do not find that this attitude precludes all moral judgment; it is not a wilful blindness but a new kind of seeing.

When we are engaged in business, in politics, in games, in the ordinary activities of daily life, it is all very real to us, but it is all transient; it passes like a dream, and when one stops to think, we can say with Napoleon, *'Il faut quitter tout çela.'* Amid the transience is nothing eternal? When I was a boy there were two houses I called home. Both have been pulled down, and not one brick remains upon another. I remember a walk when I saw, as I knew for the last time, the fields and flowers and hedges where I had wandered carefree as a boy:

> I never heard the larks so clear and sure,
>> I never saw such light upon the grass,
>>> Nor knew the hedge so drenched in blackthorn foam:
>>> Ah, these fair fields to me are part of home!
>> Today with sad and lingering steps I pass
> Down well-trod paths in lone discomfiture.

> Here I, a lad with all undimmed delight,
>> Chased the red admiral and meadow-brown,
>>> And conned the lore of bird and flower and tree;
>>> But here, returning, I next year must see
>> Street, villa, garage—an industrial town,
> Outsprawling London's latest satellite.

But has it all gone for ever 'like the bubble on the fountain, like the foam on the river'? I think not. It was transient, but it was the transient expression of some spiritual reality which is not transient. I once put the case somewhat crudely thus:

> Ah, not all passes hence;
>> Something shall stay
> Outliving transience.
>> Shoots that in May
> Break through the teeming sod
>> Fade in December,
> But that abides which God
>> Wills to remember.

Things have passed and gone; that which they signified has not. The houses have been pulled down, the fields where I saw in unreflecting wonder the buttercups, valerian and moon-daisies have become 'desirable plots' or covered with new buildings. But that which they signified is part of me, and am I, too, transient?

One must be honest with oneself as well as with others about these questions. When one has lived as long as I have, it is inevitable that many or most of those whom one has loved are no more to be seen on earth, and I have undergone the greatest bereavement which any man on earth can suffer. I can only write of that which I see or think I see. Seeing is perhaps the wrong word here; we cannot see or prove, but here as in all matters of the spirit right feeling or response is the only pathway to reality.

The whole universe, as I have put it, seems to be a kind of code, a hinting, an indication, an incarnate expression of that which lies beyond, all transient beauties a foretaste of eternal Beauty. The veil that hides the immortal world from our eyes grows thin at times.

It is often said that men 'lose' their friends by death. Such a word would not be natural to me. I have no sense of having 'lost' those whom I see no more. Curiously enough, we often more clearly see and therefore more surely possess our friends when we see them no more and they have sloughed off the infirmities that prevented them from revealing what they really meant. I should not even naturally say that I remember those who are gone, though of course I do remember them, but rather I am aware of them; by this I do not mean any sensation that is either physical or psychic; it is rather an awareness like the awareness of happiness and affection when a family after separation is reunited; it is a quiet awareness of their presences.

I have no answer to those who say that this is self-deception except that I do not wilfully deceive myself. It may be said that the memory of these persons or these past experiences has become part of me, and that when I die they will disappear with me. But shall I altogether die? I could contemplate my extinction with a certain degree of equanimity, but if I am asked to believe that the characters known to me that have been formed by patience and courage and suffering and goodness are of no ultimate significance, that Jesus Christ is dead and done for, and there is nothing more to be said about him, then my reason (I am sure it is my reason) is revolted. That does not make sense; nothing makes sense if all 'this tale of drearihead' which is the story of mankind and cosmic evolution comes to nothing in the end. If that which makes no sense in itself and for anything else be true, then let reason abdicate and all this striving and thinking be laid aside as meaningless. I cannot in my heart or with my mind believe it.

It will be remembered that I am not now offering proofs but trying to be honest with my experience, and I think that the world in which I now live, at least at those moments when I am most alive, is something like what the Fourth Evangelist means by 'eternal life'. It is a world to which time is irrelevant. When I think of the earliest days of my childhood, what I remember with more or less clarity is my toys, the nursery, my mother spinning and singing as she sang, my father's pleasure at the hypaticas in the garden, but these are, as it were, a code, like the print upon a book-page; it is a non-temporal meaning that comes over me. When I meet my friends or even strangers in the streets, their gestures, their clothes, their words, their expressions are a code through which I read with varying clarity a person, a character, an entity that is not temporal or even finite. Every object, every person is lustred with the eternal and the infinite.

155

I have written

> that abides which God
> Wills to remember.

I must use anthropomorphic language, for we have no other. We cannot think of God as having a bad memory like mine! There is a famous passage in his *Confessions* (11.10), where St Augustine writes of an ever memorable conversation with his mother shortly before she died. They were speaking of the Life itself, that which 'never comes to be but is, as it was and shall be evermore, because it is neither past nor future but present only, for it is eternal . . . and as we talked and yearned after it, we touched it for an instant with the whole force of our hearts.' I think that we all, including my agnostic friends, can from our own feebler experience understand what Augustine says. We have touched, we have been touched by, the eternal, the transcendent, the beyond, by the unimaginable, incomprehensible and mysterious Thou.

> Yet in his hand who lie
> Thus held in being for a day, shall I
> Slip from his grasp when Death's resistless flood
> Pours o'er my eyes and chills my pulsing blood,
> Fade from his memory, at one dire stroke
> Fall into Nothingness? Shall God revoke
> And stay his lovingkindness? Not in me
> Is life, nor in him death, and finally
> Whate'er an instant he vouchsafed to bless
> Must tinctured be with everlastingness.

The world in which I live, and which alone seems to me an ultimately real world, is beyond time and space or in another dimension altogether, and my attitude to it is one of quite unmeasurable thankfulness.

In gratitude and in reverence reason, as that learned logician Cook Wilson said, can only express itself emotionally. I am thankful for the gift of reason, limited though it be; I am thankful for this beauty which is neither in my eye nor in the electrons but is my direct apprehension of that which symbolizes the Beyond; I am thankful in all and beyond all for Jesus of Nazareth, whom I hold in aweful reverence, and who has declared and made credible to me an infinite Compassion at the heart of the Eternal.

In this book I have not asked my agnostic friends to abandon their agnosticism, if they are looking for any logical or scientific demonstration of things spiritual; I have asked them, rather, to accept and acknowledge as the dictates of reason those insights and principles by which they live, and further, to be honest with the figure of Jesus as it comes to us through history. I have not asked them to 'accept Christianity' if by this be understood the giving of assent to the customs, the conventions, the formulated dogmas of the churches. I have distinguished, as one must, between 'Christianity' and Christ. The great intellectual and personal insincerity to which we are all tempted is to refuse to be serious with Jesus Christ. Because of him I believe that the peace and quietness and thankfulness of which I have written are open to my agnostic friends, who now walk disconsolately in the shadows, if they will accept with their reason that which their hearts know, and this not least when they remember every day the sick and the lonely, the prisoners and the refugees, the hungry, the helpless and the oppressed.

I have argued throughout this book that it is through the physical, the material, that we become aware of the spiritual and immaterial. There is no experience, no event, through which we may not become aware of the Beyond. In that sense all Nature and all life is, or may be, sacramental, the spiritual being brought home to us through the material and physical. Jesus is a real person; he is not dead and done for. Since that last betrayal night at a turning point of human history, not a week has passed, probably not a day has passed, but Christians under one form or another, in rigorous simplicity or in gorgeous setting of art and music, have gathered round the table, and as once at Emmaus, the presence of their Lord has been made known to them in 'the breaking of the bread'. It is to that table that I would summon my dear agnostic friends.

DATE DUE			